UNDERSTANDING AND IMPLEMENTING INCLUSION IN MUSEUMS

UNDERSTANDING AND IMPLEMENTING INCLUSION IN MUSEUMS

Laura-Edythe Coleman

ROWMAN & LITTLEFIELD
Lanham • Boulder • New York • London

Published by Rowman & Littlefield
A wholly owned subsidiary of
The Rowman & Littlefield Publishing Group, Inc.
4501 Forbes Boulevard, Suite 200, Lanham, Maryland 20706
www.rowman.com

Unit A, Whitacre Mews, 26-34 Stannary Street, London SE11 4AB

British Library Cataloguing in Publication Information Available

Library of Congress Cataloging-in-Publication Data Available

ISBN 9781538110515 (cloth : alk. paper)
ISBN 9781538110812 (pbk. : alk. paper)
ISBN 9781538110829 (electronic)

∞™ The paper used in this publication meets the minimum requirements of
American National Standard for Information Sciences—Permanence of Paper
for Printed Library Materials, ANSI/NISO Z39.48-1992.

Printed in the United States of America

For Emily,
You are the theory of everything.

Contents

Figures

Preface

Understanding and Implementing Inclusion in Museums is the first text to focus solely on the notion of social inclusion for museums. This book is intended to demystify the much-debated idea of *inclusion* for museum professionals, theorists, professors, and researchers. Despite the increased interest in the concept of inclusive museums, we have very little tangible understanding of the term. This book provides that understanding in a concise and complete manner.

We have heard countless times that inclusion is a good thing for museums. The word has permeated our professional conversations, conferences, and publications. Inclusion is even now considered by the American Alliance of Museums (AAM) to be one of the core institutional values of the twenty-first-century museum. While AAM released definitions for diversity and inclusion in February 2014 with its updated Diversity and Inclusion Policy, these descriptions merely introduced the term *inclusion* into the vocabulary of the field, without providing clear definitions. The AAM statement is likely to have significant long-term consequences for the field, notably impacting (1) the museum (re)accreditation process; (2) professional practice; and (3) vocational training. In the wake of this AAM statement, museum professionals of all levels are left uncertain as to the meaning of *inclusion*, and they are ill equipped to implement inclusion in their museums.

Understanding and Implementing Inclusion in Museums will be the definitive theory- and application-based practitioner guidebook for implementing inclusion in museums for the foreseeable future. But what do we mean by inclusion? Why do we need inclusion? Is it a good thing? Who or what are we including? If you are confused by all of these discussions, you are not alone. I wrote this book to answer the many questions that I have received over the recent years about inclusion for museums.

Understanding and Implementing Inclusion in Museums serves as the first-of-its-kind text on the concept of *inclusion*. In this book, I will explore the multiple theoretical, historical, and practical meanings of the term *inclusion*. The chapters within this book are intended to function as a guide for understanding and implementing inclusion in your museum. In the first chapter, I make a case for inclusion in American museums by discussing how our museums are not inclusive spaces, but rather institutions of exclusion. I develop early in the book, within chapter 2, a working definition for the term *inclusion* based on both theory and history. I highlight the incredible potential that inclusion has to expand the social role of the museum—a task that has been assigned to the American museum field for several decades. In chapter 3 I explore the significant advantages of inclusion theory application in museums. In order to formulate your own opinion of inclusion, I have outlined the advantages and disadvantages of inclusion for museums. Aided by inclusion theory, museum professionals can be reassured that their museums will reveal exclusion and develop lasting solutions to problems of marginalization and discrimination in their communities.

To implement inclusion efficiently in our museums, I have outlined and expanded on a three-tiered spectrum of inclusion, first pioneered by Richard Sandell in 1998. The vast majority of American institutions are along the lower end of this inclusivity spectrum. As museums progress along the spectrum of inclusivity, their impacts become greater upon society. Chapter 4 focuses almost exclusively on the first tier of inclusivity: the relationship a museum may have with an individual. For museums to cultivate relationships with their individual visitors, they must focus on particular components of this relationship.

One hundred years have passed since museum founder and librarian extraordinaire John Cotton Dana proposed that American museums and libraries should be relevant to the communities in which they reside. The time has come for American museums to partner with community programs for the benefit of society. Chapter 5 outlines the second tier of the inclusive museum, aiding in social regeneration: partnerships with programs, agencies, and community organizations. For many museum professionals, the prospect of community partnerships is unnerving at best and unwelcome at worst. Chapter 5 explores why there are hindrances to partnerships with community organizations and how we can transform our perspectives while staying true to our mission statements. Included throughout this chapter are examples of successful museum–community agency partnerships.

Chapter 6 examines the highly contested notion of the museum as a propulsion agent for social change. Examples are presented of museums that, acting as change agents, have debunked the myth of museum neutrality. The two main types of museums in this third tier are analyzed: first, those born with a social agenda; second, those that adopt a social agenda. In response to the dire situation, that American museums are not prepared to implement inclusion, I have compiled from successful cases of inclusion a collection of tools for surveying, analyzing, and implementation. In chapter 7, I present the practical guide to implementing inclusion within your museum. I also provide steps for implementing the inclusive practice and a clear pathway to progress through the spectrum of inclusivity.

As museums grapple with their new social role and the application of inclusive practices, we will begin to see a higher demand for evaluation processes. In chapter 8, I deliver detailed procedures for successfully evaluating the inclusivity of your museum. I arm you with a series of evaluative techniques based on social science research methods and the national standards of EU/UK policies on social inclusion. I will also demonstrate blended approaches, melding American sensibility with a Western European metric, ultimately producing a uniquely American set of tools for evaluating inclusion in our museums.

Chapter 9 highlights several of those individuals who are acting as advocates of inclusion, being agents of inclusive practice, and those designing the architecture of inclusion for American museums. On the spectrum of participation, many individuals are advocates for inclusive practices, some are also agents of social change, and only a few are *true architects* of inclusion for American museums.

Finally, in chapter 10, I issue a challenge to the museum field in general, and to the American museum field in particular: *understand and implement inclusion now*. Although this book is written from an American perspective, with specific applications to American museums, I draw upon the more considerable body of research and experience of our UK museum colleagues.

We have never had a book solely about inclusion for museums, and never with such a strong focus on American institutions. I invite you to join the conversation concerning inclusion armed with greater understanding and the tools to implement change through your museum.

Acknowledgments

In isolation, I would have written nothing. I am grateful for those who have listened to my thoughts, been brave enough to banter with me, and provided the much-needed feedback to write this book.

Charles Harmon and Rowman & Littlefield, thank you kindly for the opportunity to write this text and to speak to my colleagues through the power of print.

Dr. Porchia Moore, thank you for the many intense conversations that we have shared concerning inclusion for museums.

I am grateful for the many museum theorists and practitioners in whose steps I follow: the Inclusive Museum Conference and Knowledge Community, the Incluseum, the American Alliance of Museums, the International Committee of Museums, the International Committee of Memorial Museums, Professor Richard Sandell, Professor Robert Janes, Professor Anwar Tlili, Karen Franklin, and Ophelia Leon of ICMEMO.

I often wrote in Catalina Cafe, and I thank Rachel, Micah, and Brooke.

Chris Pascoe and Patrick Pierson, thank you for hosting my writing sabbatical in London—your kindness was instrumental to my success.

Navigating the narrow channels of academia is difficult, and I appreciate Professor Paul Marty for his continued support of my endeavors.

Nothing in life happens without a dare to dream. I thank Vincent Hunt for daring me to envision a better world.

Robin Felty, thank you for your continued friendship and kindness.

Tina Neace, you have always been here for me—thank you.

I am forever thankful for my friendship with the brilliant researcher, Dr. Abby Phillips.

Rebecca Reibman, thank you kindly for providing your home as an oasis for writing.

Professor Schrödinger and research assistant Maddi Lynn, thank you for exceptional support of my work.

Daniel, my rocket man, I am so proud of you.
Joe, my passionate chef, I am so proud of you.
Zach, my logical son, I am so proud of you.
Emily, my whimsical daughter, I am so proud of you.

Dearest Chuck, thank you for being my partner; as in all things, this book is as much yours as it is mine.

1

Why Do Museums Need Inclusion?

Over the last several years, the American museum professional field has been energized around the word *inclusion*. You may have heard the term and want inclusion for your museum. But why do museums need inclusion? Why are we driven as a field to embrace and implement inclusion—a term that we know little about? It is all too easy to be caught up in the fervor of new terminology without understanding why (or even *if*) we need inclusion for museums.

Why do museums need inclusion? In short, we crave inclusion because American museums are exclusive and excluding spaces. Every recent statistic brought forward by the Center for the Future of Museums has reported the exclusiveness of American museums (Center for the Future of Museums 2010). There is conclusive evidence that American museums, as institutions, have not echoed the democratic nature of our nation. Quite simply, our museums are not "by the people, for the people" (Lincoln 1863). In fact, quite the opposite is true: if American museums are for the people, it is often only for certain elite people. How can this be? Truly, we are twenty years past the moment in which Stephen Weil summarized the shift in museums from being "about something to being for somebody" (Weil 2002). I argue that although museums are for somebody, they are not yet for everybody.

American Museums Are Currently Exclusive and Excluding Spaces

How are American museums exclusive? I use the term *exclusive* to describe the inherent nature of our museums to be places for the elite, the fashionable, the educated, and the wealthy. The term *exclusive* describes a scenario of discrimination and segregation. In what ways are American museums exclusive spaces? First, American museums struggle to be culturally responsive and inclusive of their entire community. Second, as institutions, American museums are hesitant to form partnerships with social organizations and agencies that have similar but still different mission statements. Third, American museums refuse to become the conduit or platform for broad social change. These points are harsh—a hard truth for us as American museum professionals to bear, and, hopefully, we are urged to look for inclusive solutions to our problems.

American Museums Are Not Culturally Inclusive

American museums are far from inclusive—especially regarding museum visitor demographics. In 2010, the Center for the Future of Museums reported that there is a widening gulf between the national population and museum visitor demographics (Center for the Future of Museums 2010). The national population data was drawn from the census, performed every ten years within the United States. The museum visitor demographics were compared against the national population changes in the United States. As demonstrated in figure 1.1, the current minority population of the United States is 34 percent and is expected to grow to 46 percent over the next twenty-five years. American museums report a mere 9 percent minority population in their annual attendance figures.

If the numerical data is not impressive enough, there is a growing body of anecdotal evidence to support the notion that

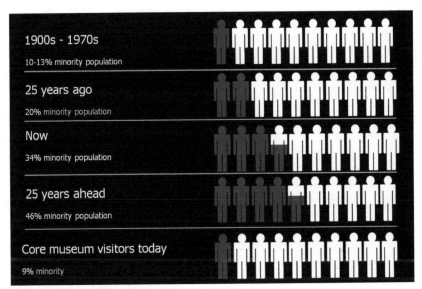

Figure 1.1.   Museum Figures.
US Census Bureau, Reach Advisors.

American museums are exclusive institutions. Studies dating back to the 1980s have linked low museum attendance by minority populations to "subtle forms of exclusion" (Dimaggio and Ostrower 1990, 753–78). This exclusivity in other American organizations—schools, for example—would be termed discrimination. This problem is rampant and denounced by many, including former First Lady Michelle Obama. During her remarks at the opening of the Whitney Museum on April 30, 2015, Mrs. Obama spoke of her disconnect from museums due to the long-standing marginalization of African Americans: "You see, there are so many kids in this country who look at places like museums and concert halls and other cultural centers, and they think to themselves, well, that's not a place for me, for someone who looks like me, for someone who comes from my neighborhood" (Obama 2015). When the wife of your nation's leader cannot see herself in an American museum, we must acknowledge both as museum professionals and as Americans that there are significant levels of exclusion (discrimination) occurring within our museums.

Figure 1.2.   Michelle Obama at the Opening of the Whitney Museum.
Filip Wolack, courtesy of the Whitney Museum.

American Museums Are Hesitant to Form Partnerships with Social Organizations and Agencies

American museums provide significant value to their communities (Scott 2013). This value is often found to benefit the local economy and strengthen public education. Museums could partner more often with social agencies to provide physical and mental health benefits; yet they do not. Why? The main anecdote provided by museums concerning their hesitancy to form partnerships with other agencies is "mission purity" (Jacobsen 2014, 1–18). American museums are concerned that their main mission, a statement unique to their institution, will be neglected should resources be allocated to another endeavor. The other agencies are viewed as competitive, no matter how complementary, to the mission statement of those museums.

American Museums Refuse to Become the Conduit or Platform for Broad Social Change

The vast majority of American museum professionals do not envision their museum as a space to instigate broad social change. For many museum professionals, the idea of taking a stand for or against anything in a museum is repugnant. Why? Because the myth of museum neutrality still exists. American museum professionals and the general public revere museums as neutral zones—places where politics are off limits (Murawski 2017c). Perhaps most American museum professionals recognize this fallacy; yet they hold on to the superstition that museums are spaces hidden from the harsh reality of life. Only a small minority of museum professionals dares to speak loudly about this myth, a reflection, perhaps, of the American museum as an institution.

Why Does Our Nation Need Inclusive Museums?

It is an understatement to say that we live in divisive and turbulent times in America. The events of solely the past five years have revealed the deep racial divide still abiding in America. Public battles have been waged over the removal of Confederate statues in the Southeast, the 2017 Charlottesville protests being most prominent (Fortin 2017). Similar battles have been waged regarding the flying of the Confederate flag at government buildings and the killing of black men by police, such as in Ferguson (Bonilla and Rosa 2015, 4–17; Phillip 2015). These arguments have boiled over to produce riots and violence in America (Buchanan 2014). Nationalist fervor has resulted in harsh feelings toward immigrants and foreigners. All of these recent events can be tackled by museums through inclusive practices. Our museums are called to be culturally responsive. What's more, we need to be more than responsive; we need to initiate cultural inclusion. The American museum community has been criticized for not responding quickly (if at all) to these devastating events (Paquet Kinsley, Wittman, and Moore 2014). I argue that through inclusion we have the ability to preemptively initiate inclusion in our society. Instead of taking a reactive stance to the events as they unfold, museums have the ability to impact society in advance. Our museums have a responsibility to live up to "the growing belief among practitioners, policymakers, and the public alike in the power of museums to inspire hope and healing, improve lives, and better the world" (Silverman 2010). We must accept that responsibility and commit to becoming agents of social change (Sandell 1998, 401–18).

Inclusion Is More Than a Buzzword

American museums have the opportunity to use inclusion if they recognize it as more than a mere buzzword. As practitioners, we love buzzwords and phrases, but such language can obscure the true power of the idea behind the word. We must realize that inclusion is powerful, not because the word is popular in American museum professional discourse, but because it represents struggle, the battle to end exclusion and discrimination. What evidence exists to promote inclusion as the preferred theory of museum practice? In this book I will examine the growing number of cases, studies, and reports of inclusive practices globally. The social role of the museum is "more than simply a passing phase," and American museum practitioners must adapt inclusive practices now (Weil 2002).

We Have Tried Other Methods and Failed

We have tried other methods of tackling exclusion and marginalization in our museums, and they simply have not worked. As I will discuss in chapter 3, inclusion goes beyond our discussions of traditional notions such as diversity and multiculturalism. These methods fail our museums in several ways, and in turn our museums do not live up to their potential in society. In chapter 3 I will discuss in detail the advantages inclusion theory has over traditional frameworks such as diversity and multiculturalism. Implemented correctly, inclusion can effect change where diversity and multiculturalism fail.

We Have a Unique Opportunity

American museum professionals have the unique opportunity to implement, evaluate, and articulate inclusive practices for our museums and in doing so expect real social change. Museums exist to be in "the service of society and its development," and the professionals who work within those museums are charged with the mission to serve society (International Council of Museums 2007). Inclusive practice assists both museum professionals in their mission to serve society and museums in their mission to create real social change.

2

The Spectrum of Inclusive Theories for Museums

Inclusion is not a single achievable point. Often, I am asked, "How will we know that our museum is inclusive?" And, well, this question does get to the idea of evaluation of museums—for example, is my museum performing as it should? All questions about evaluating inclusiveness should wait until we have a firm understanding of the possible definitions of inclusion. In other words, museum professionals cannot embark on the evaluation phase of understanding inclusion until we have developed sufficient vocabulary concerning inclusion—simply to talk among ourselves coherently. To this end, I will address evaluation later in this book, in chapter 8, "Tools for Evaluating Inclusion in Your Museum." Evaluation is important to this conversation, but we may not address it until we have sorted the vocabulary issues out.

We will first detangle the notion of inclusion by examining the historical frameworks of the term. As museum professionals better understand the roots of inclusion, we will be more capable of applying inclusion theory to our museums. *Inclusion*, in American terminology, and the related concept of *social inclusion* (in UK/EU terminology), originated from a deeper historical relationship with the idea of social exclusion (Coleman 2016a; Rawal 2008; Sandell 1998, 401–18). In this chapter, I will trace the ancestry of the term *inclusion*.

A Definition of *Inclusion*

The term *inclusion* is ambiguous at best. Surrounding and permeating the myriad of professional and theoretical museum debates of today is the grim reality that we have not agreed upon an understanding of the word *inclusion*. "What is inclusion?" I have been asked this question many times, and quite frankly no one has ever been satisfied, much less happy, with my definition. What I can say about inclusion is deeply rooted in my understanding of museum history, theory, and philosophy—and yet my words are, in no way, definitive. My working definition is "social inclusion for museums: (verb) The process by which museums combat social exclusion through cultural, social, political, and economic means" (see figure 2.1). I would very much like to give you a precise definition of inclusion. Sadly, I cannot give you this—instead, this text is meant to guide you, the museum practitioner, in a series of self-reflective exercises to your

Social Inclusion for museums (verb):

"The process by which museums combat social exclusion through cultural, social, political, and economic means."

Figure 2.1. Social Inclusion for Museums Defined.

Created by Laura-Edythe Coleman.

understanding of inclusion. Let us examine the roles we have in inclusionary, and by default exclusionary, museum practices.

First, inclusion is not a singular concept—we can define inclusion in multiple ways, and this notion leads to the use of a spectrum: if inclusion is not a single achievable point, then it may exist with some flexibility along a spectrum of possibilities. We will discuss this flexibility more in chapter 3, "The Advantages and Disadvantages of Inclusion for Museums." For now, let us consider that inclusion is a highly subjective notion and accept that, like others before us, it will appear along the spectrum that we will discuss (Coleman 2016a; Dodd and Sandell 2001; Sandell 1998). Understandably, to have a term with multiple definitions can be unnerving, but we must first acknowledge those multiple meanings, and that will assist you, as a museum professional, in creating an informed definition of inclusion to which you will eventually subscribe.

How did we arrive at this term *inclusion*? All good definitions have a historical basis, and this word *inclusion* has a lineage within our language. Most recently, the term *inclusion* crept into American museum practitioner circles at the turn of the twenty-first century (Coleman 2015; Coleman and Moore forthcoming). In American museum dialogues, we link *inclusion* with the word *diversity*, and we often invoke the term *inclusion* in conversations concerning racism, equality, equity, and social justice (Moore 2014). For many American museum professionals who have seen decades of change in museum discourse, the term *inclusion* is used interchangeably with *diversity* or *multiculturalism*. But as I will discuss later in this book, inclusion has several theoretical and practical advantages to both diversity and multiculturalism (Moore 2014). I distinguish between inclusion, diversity, and multiculturalism and do not see these terms as synonymous despite their usage in such a fashion by our peers. One purpose in writing this book is to address, early on, the distinction between inclusion and other theories in the hope that these terms will not become formally equated.

Inclusion officially appeared in American museum practitioner discourse in 2014, in AAM's policy on "Diversity and Inclusion" (American Alliance of Museums "Diversity and Inclusion Policy"). Despite the intense interest generated by the public release of this statement, we understand little about inclusion in the United States. AAM's definition of inclusion, while well meaning, was drafted verbatim from an earlier definition of inclusion by the nonprofit organization the United Way (United Way "Diversity and Inclusion"). This definition, which begins "inclusion: the act of including," does little to illuminate the actual reason for inclusion, and without that reasoning, the definition falls flat (American Alliance of Museums "Diversity and Inclusion Policy"). By this, I mean that because this definition lacks any reference to the antithesis of inclusion (exclusion) that it fundamentally misses the point of the term altogether.

The Ambiguous Nature of Inclusion: A Definition of Inclusion Begins with Exclusion

Inclusion is the "assumed corollary" to exclusion, and it is conceptualized solely in relation to exclusion (Rawal 2008, 172). In this perspective, social inclusion and exclusion are "inseparable sides of the same coin" (Rawal 2008, 172). Museum professionals must understand that inclusion is not a stand-alone concept. In explaining this basic abstract conceptual relationship, I often ask museum practitioners to attempt a definition of the word *good* without any reference to *evil*. The notion of "good" is inseparable from that of "evil." Therefore, in determining a definition of *inclusion*, we must reference its antithesis—*exclusion* (Rawal 2008). Discourse on inclusion in the United Kingdom and European Union often contains descriptors such as *combating* or *mitigating* social exclusion—an active and thoughtful response to exclusion (Rawal 2008).

So inclusion is a response to exclusion? Yes. But what is exclusion? Is there exclusion in the United States? Yes, but before we examine exclusion in the United States, we must account for the prominent use of the terms *inclusion* and *exclusion* in UK practitioner discourse (Rawal 2008). Before the UK usage of exclusion, museum practitioners in Western Europe used the term extensively. In fact, the epicenter for this term is France in 1970 (Rawal 2008).

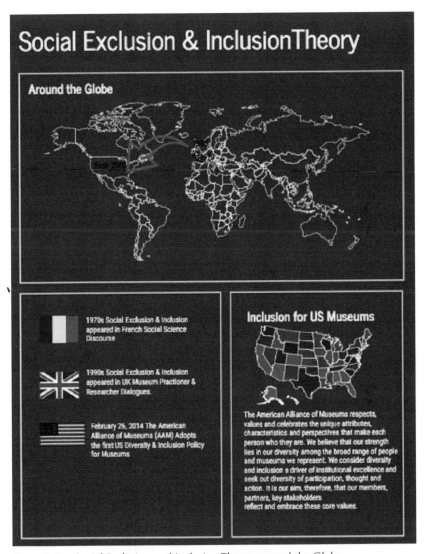

Social Exclusion & InclusionTheory

Around the Globe

Best 2000

Inclusion for US Museums

1970s Social Exclusion & Inclusion appeared in French Social Science Discourse

1990s Social Exclusion & Inclusion appeared in UK Museum Practioner & Researcher Dialogues.

February 26, 2014 The American Alliance of Museums (AAM) Adopts the first US Diversity & Inclusion Policy for Museums

The American Alliance of Museums respects, values and celebrates the unique attributes, characteristics and perspectives that make each person who they are. We believe that our strength lies in our diversity among the broad range of people and museums we represent. We consider diversity and inclusion a driver of institutional excellence and seek out diversity of participation, thought and action. It is our aim, therefore, that our members, partners, key stakeholders reflect and embrace these core values.

Figure 2.2.   Social Exclusion and Inclusion Theory around the Globe.
Created by Laura-Edythe Coleman.

Historical Relationship with the Term *Exclusion*

During the 1970s, France expanded its welfare system, and numerous previously ignored exclusionary practices came to light (Rawal 2008). *Social exclusion* became the term used to describe economic woes and social injustices. Why France? Why did exclusion/inclusion as we know it today originate in France? Well, the origins of exclusion have been traced to three possible distinctly French paradigms: solidarity, specialization, and monopoly (Silver 1994, 531). The notion of solidarity arises from an intense devotion to French republicanisms and the writings of Rousseau (Silver 1994). From the solidarity viewpoint, exclusion is seen as a breakdown in the unity of society—a practice that is dangerous not only to the excluded individual but also to society as a whole (Silver 1994, 531). The concept of specialization addresses the cultural and political pluralism in modern Western democracies—both the capacity for great enlightenment through specialization and the concurrent creation of exclusive practices. In specialization, individuals are members of societal spheres that denote politics, culture, education, skills, and more. These societal spheres may interact, overlap, or be extremely isolated from one another. The degree to which an individual can cross the barriers between specialized spheres is commonly conceived in commercial imagery: "social capital" or "cultural currency" (Silver 1994, 531). When the barriers between spheres are too difficult to cross, specialization is considered a negative, harmful problem, most often termed *discrimination*. In the paradigm of monopoly, exclusion is the tension between classes, for power and for obtaining a monopoly on resources. Monopoly is deeply entrenched in the concepts of social democracy and conflict theory, and it is based on Marx and Weber (Silver 1994).

Expansion of Inclusion/Exclusion Theory Globally

As exclusion theory expanded beyond France, research and practitioner dialogue served to evolve the theory, adapting

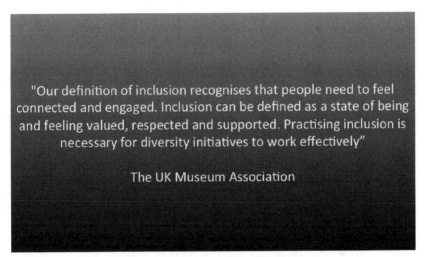

Figure 2.3. UK Museums Association Definition of Inclusion.
Created by Laura-Edythe Coleman, derived from UK Museums Association 2014.

it to changing times (Tlili 2008, 123–47). By the late 1990s, exclusion, as a concept relevant to UK museums, had been crystallized into distinct components (Sandell 2003, 45–62). (See figure 2.3.)

Richard Sandell, professor and researcher at the University of Leicester, created a format for examining social exclusion as well as a typology for the understanding of social inclusion within museums. In "Museums as Agents of Social Inclusion," Sandell proposed that social exclusion is a multifaceted problem that negatively affects the social, economic, political, and cultural life of both the individual and society (Sandell 1998). Please see Sandell's chart (figure 2.4) for the depiction of these four components (social, economic, political, cultural) as they relate to the museum.

We see the social element of exclusion when an individual lacks the social opportunities as afforded by a strong relationship with society. Economic exclusion frequently occurs—especially in US museums that charge hefty admission prices. Economic exclusion further happens when transportation to a museum is costly—a situation that occurs commonly in the United States due

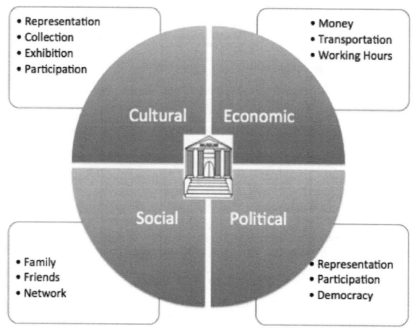

Figure 2.4. Sandell's Typology of Social Exclusion.
Created by Laura-Edythe Coleman, derived from Sandell 1998.

to the vast geography of the nation. Larger museums are located in cities, with much of the country in suburban or rural areas. For many Americans, part of the economic problem is the sheer distance from locations and a complete lack of public transportation.

Political exclusion occurs at a structural level in American museums. Time after time, US museums are called out for their lack of diversity in their exhibits, in their collections, and their staffs—particularly in leadership positions. This exclusion has a compounding impact as those who are marginalized become less likely to participate in the political process—in effect, political exclusion in museums upholds the status quo and diminishes the voices of those already marginalized.

Lastly, there is cultural exclusion. Really? Yes. Even in our cultural institutions there exists cultural exclusion. How can our museums be for all Americans if they do not represent all Americans? We must acknowledge that how we represent cultures and how we include communities in the making of exhibits directly influences the inclusivity/exclusivity of our museums. Are there other aspects of exclusion? Sure—but the format described by Sandell is an excellent place to begin our serious conversation concerning exclusion. As we review the myriad of inclusive museum practices in this book, keep in mind Sandell's format for examining exclusion within your museum. You may find that not all of these types of exclusion are present in your museum, or that your museum may need to focus more heavily on one aspect of exclusion. For example, you may evaluate your museum and discover that cultural exclusion is not the most troublesome but that the admission fees are cost prohibitive. Or the opposite may be true: your museum is free to the public, but your museum mostly displays artifacts from white settlers and neglects the stories and objects of indigenous peoples.

All of this discussion of exclusion is to bring you, the museum professional, to the point at which you can now formulate a definition of inclusion for yourself—in relation to this understanding of exclusion. Inclusion is more than just "the act of including"; it is the practices that mitigate exclusion. In effect, inclusion is the action that cancels out or nullifies or lessens the impacts of exclusion. What is inclusion? Inclusion is the conscientiously applied effort to combat exclusion within our society.

A Spectrum of Inclusive Museums

Now that we understand inclusion and its historical relationship with exclusion, how do we apply it to museums? The first task is to consider where your museum is now: Look at the spectrum of inclusivity outlined in Sandell's typology (see figure 2.5). Where does your museum fit on this typology now? Where do you want your museum to be? I encourage museums to progress along Sandell's continuous spectrum. The typology is designed to "illustrate a change in museums—an increasing desire to make clear the museum's social purpose and the value it provides in relation to addressing contemporary social issues" (Sandell 1998, 401–18). The three categories of in-

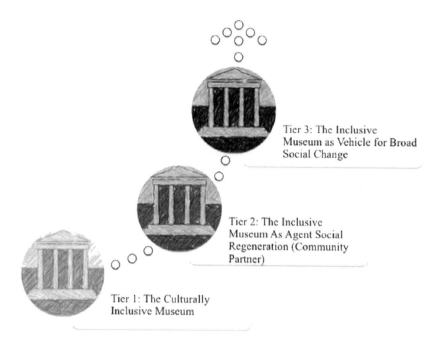

Figure 2.5.   Sandell's Spectrum of the Inclusive Museum.
Created by Laura-Edythe Coleman, derived from Sandell 1998.

stitutions present in the typology are "the inclusive museum," "the museum as an agent of social regeneration," and "the museum as the vehicle for broad social change" (Sandell 1998). Each of these types of museums has different goals, methods, and levels of transparency. As a consequence, the possible measurement of the impact of the socially inclusive museum does well to begin with an understanding of the levels of impact suggested by Sandell's typology.

Tier 1: The Culturally Inclusive Museum

The first tier of social inclusive museum types is the inclusive museum. This kind of museum has goals to represent marginalized groups in exhibits and to provide access for those excluded due to lack of transportation or wealth. This primary level of the

Tier 1: The Culturally Inclusive Museum

*The goal of this museum is to "achieve cultural inclusion"

*This goal is achieved through the "representation of and participation and access for those excluded."

*Social exclusion is therefore "addressed indirectly."

*This type of inclusion is created by forming *partnerships with people*

*And leverages collections, exhibits and programming to produce exhibits that are *personal, participatory, and portable*.

Figure 2.6.   *Tier 1: The Culturally Inclusive Museum.*
Created by Laura-Edythe Coleman, derived from Sandell 1998.

socially inclusive museum will prioritize the inclusion of objects and exhibits that represent the marginalized portions of their society. Additionally, the socially inclusive museum will engage those disenfranchised groups in a participatory and collaborative way, thus assuring access to museum exhibits.

Tier 2: The Museum as Agent of Social Regeneration

The second category of the socially inclusive museum is the museum as an agent of social regeneration. This type of museum connects with the community on more than the cultural level. An institution functioning as an agent of social regeneration integrates cultural exhibits with social, economic, and political aspects of communities. A museum acting as an agent of social regeneration

Tier 2: The Inclusive Museum As Agent of Social Regeneration (Community Partner)

*The goal of this museum is to "improve individuals' quality of life."

*This goal is achieved through "providing a forum for public debate, education, and persuasion."

*Social exclusion may be addressed directly through *partnerships with community agencies, organizations, and programs*

*And leverages collections, exhibits, and programming to produce exhibits *that place the health and well-being of the community first,*

*Through *democratic processes* that require *time,*

*And creates *relationships with the community that are more important that results*

Figure 2.7.   Tier 2: The Inclusive Museum as Agent of Social Regeneration.
Created by Laura-Edythe Coleman, as derived from Sandell 1998.

would present public initiatives to better the lives of the individuals within a community. An example of such initiatives in museum exhibits would be one that works in collaboration with community organizations such as the local health department. Several example successful collaborations are in chapter 9, "Advocates, Agents, and Architects for American Museums."

Tier 3: The Museum as the Vehicle for Broad Social Change

The museum as the vehicle for broad social change is the third museum type in Sandell's typology. This museum acknowledges publicly its societal role, determined to change society for the better. As a vehicle for broad social change, this museum type influences society by a social inclusion agenda. According to Sandell, "Those museums which clearly articulate their

Tier 3: The Inclusive Museum as the Vehicle for Broad Social Change

*The goal of this museum is to "influence society, and instigate positive social change."

*This goal is achieved through the "initiatives which seek to alleviate disadvantage and encourage personal development."

*Social exclusion is therefore directly and the inclusive role of the museum is *expressed clearly in the museum's mission and vision statements.*

*This type of inclusion is created by the *sharing of curatorial authority,*

*And leverages collections, exhibits and programming to produce exhibits that are *take an institutional stand against exclusion within society.*

Figure 2.8. Tier 3: The Inclusive Museum as the Vehicle for Broad Social Change. Created by Laura-Edythe Coleman, as derived from Sandell 1998.

purpose in relation to society and which purposefully seek to position themselves as organisations with a part to play in multi-agency solutions for tackling social exclusion are nevertheless still rare" (Sandell 1998, 401–18).

Museums will not, overnight, become vehicles for broad social change. The transformation will take time. The spectrum outlined in figure 2.5 will assist you in making measurable progress toward becoming an inclusive institution that benefits all of your community.

American Lenses for Viewing Inclusion: A Note on the Evolution of the Vocabulary: *Social Inclusion* versus *Inclusion*

What is the difference between *social inclusion* and *inclusion*? Why do some practitioners emphasize *inclusion* without the term *social*? Historically, there is little difference between social inclusion and inclusion. The use of the term *inclusion* solo appears to be a matter of preference. But why is there a desire to drop the word *social*? American museum professionals, unlike their UK/EU counterparts, tend to have a negative reaction to the term *social*. This is perhaps a problem inherent to Americans in general: an imposed theory containing the term *social* is indicative, in the minds of most Americans, of socialism. Although the museum practitioners I spoke to did not want to go officially on record for their views, they indicated that the term *social* was too strongly linked to *socialism* and, by default, *communism*. Viewed from this perspective, it seems a natural evolution of the term *social inclusion* to drop the word *social* and thus adapt the theory to American museum culture.

Varying Viewpoints on Inclusion for American Museum Professionals

American museum professionals, researchers, and theorists have a variety of views concerning the exact meaning of *inclusion*. The nature of the term *inclusion* is subjective, and disagreements concerning the abstract notion of inclusion are common. Porchia Moore and others consider inclusion "commitment; an action; a continuous inquiry" and a "verb" (Coleman et al. 2016). Yet these descriptions do not seem to satisfy American museum professionals. In 2014, the American Alliance of Museums officially linked inclusion with diversity ("Diversity and Inclusion Policy"). Viewed from the perspective of AAM, museums must now look closer at the levels of ethnic diversity among their staffs and leadership. Proponents of linking diversity with inclusion cite the studies of museum personnel conducted by organizations such as the Center for the Future of Museums (2015) and the Association of Art Museum Directors (Schonfeld et al. 2015). Not everyone agrees with the linkage of inclusion and diversity (Moore 2014). Others view inclusion as a matter of social justice (Paquet Kinsley and Wittman 2016). I see inclusion as a separate concept from diversity and as the necessary platform for successful social justice (Coleman 2015). Yuha Jung sees hindrances to US museums becoming agents of social change because they are often a part of the larger societal structure built on racism and oppression (Jung 2016, 41–50).

Ultimately, as American museum professionals, we need to recognize that there are different lenses for viewing the history of the term *inclusion*. The United States has legacies of racial injustices, oppression, and slavery. These legacies differ from those of the United Kingdom and European Union and modify the format of inclusion—and even impact how we, as museum professionals, talk about inclusivity.

Inclusion Has Evolved and Will Continue to Change

The term *inclusion* has evolved in presentation as it migrated to the United States—for instance, in the elimination of the word *social* in its usage. Inclusion has also matured, at a fundamental level, by the application in the United States, an environment thick with legacies of oppression. As museum professionals, we must ask the deeper question: What else must change about the nature of inclusion to adapt it to American museums? Despite the differences of opinion among museum professionals and theorists, several points of agreement can be reached: one, that museums are not living up to their potential as agents of change; and two, that museums will need to work progressively to shed not just the skin but also the structure of exclusionary practices. How we push for change, and how quickly that change comes about in American museums, are matters that we often disagree upon. In order to formulate your own opinion of inclusion, I have provided the next chapter, "The Advantages and Disadvantages of Inclusion for Museums."

3

The Advantages and Disadvantages of Inclusion for Museums

The Advantages of Inclusion for Museums

All too often, American museum professionals are skeptical about the concept of inclusion. At conferences, museum professionals bombard me with questions such as "Inclusion? Isn't that just the latest buzzword?" or "Is this actually a new thing? . . . I mean, come on!" Or my personal favorite: "We're inclusive! We're a public museum! Anyone can visit! We don't exclude people!" However, as a profession, *we are not inclusive*—or we would not be so wound up by this term. Want to raise the blood pressure of every museum professional in a room? Ask them to tell you three specific ways that their museum is inclusive. What I have found, on a very practical level, is that discussions about inclusion challenge us to extend our conversations beyond notions of diversity, accessibility, and multiculturalism.

Advantage 1: The Expansion of the Social Role of the Museum

I wholeheartedly approve the use of inclusion theory for museums, but I know that I should present to you an unbiased opinion (if possible). Let us first begin with the advantages of inclusion theory for museums. The primary advantage of inclusion theory for museums: *expansion of the museums' role in society*. The expansion of museums' role allows us to engage more deeply with society on the issues of race, gender, sexuality, politics, religion, and more! No singular theory previously applied to our institutions allows for museums to act this substantially as agents of social change. Is it the case that your museum cannot or is not acting as an agent of social change? No, not necessarily. Rather, consider that inclusion theory will allow you to better articulate that inclusive role to your stakeholders. However fantastic your museum is now, it can only be made better by the application of inclusion theory. As you apply inclusion to your museum (see chapters 7 and 8 for examples), you will involve both internal and external communities in a dialogue of discovery. We know that we must have these difficult conversations about injustice, inequity, and more. And we understand that we must have a framework for these discussions. Inclusion is and will provide that framework for your museum. We cannot force people to change, we cannot move museums to act, but *we can alter the way we communicate*. When we create an inclusive dialogue, then change can happen—a change that is acceptable to all.

Advantage 2: The Support of the Role of Community Self-Curation

How does inclusion expand our traditional discussions of diversity and multiculturalism? Social inclusion asserts the importance of including more than representations of marginalized communities, but also engaging marginalized communities in the co-creation of community heritage exhibits. Traditional approaches to community representation include diversity, in which participants celebrate cultural differences and in which the museum curates the differences and similarities between cultures (Sandell and Nightingale 2012). Social inclusion supports the role of community self-curation, the engagement of culturally sensitive materials, and the amplification of the role of museum professionals as facilitators in cultural dialogue. Nightingale and Sandell explore the interwoven nature of inclusion, equality, diversity, and social justice and acknowledge the role of the traditional museum as "often operated in ways which exclude, marginalize and oppress"

(Sandell and Nightingale 2012). They propose that "there is growing support (and evidence) for the idea that museums can contribute towards more just, equitable and fair societies" (Sandell and Nightingale 2012). Social inclusion theory, therefore, applied conscientiously to museums, moves beyond traditional discussions of diversity and multiculturalism and enters the realm of social justice and equality. Although Sandell and Nightingale write from a UK perspective, there is little reason to doubt the efficacy of the UK inclusion applications in a US context. In short, all indicators, based on UK evaluations, suggest that inclusion can further museums in their contributions to a more just society.

How does inclusion extend the traditional talks once framed by diversity or multiculturalism? In essence, the modern notion of diversity is one that celebrates (and enforces) difference. There are multiple problems with diversity as a framework for museum practice. Porchia Moore presents diversity as a dangerous hegemonic tool that upholds traditional exclusionary practices (Moore 2014). By contrast, inclusion supports self-representation by individuals and communities. In museums using inclusion, museum professionals do not cull communities for art and objects, carefully curating differences between cultures. Instead, art/artists/communities define themselves through inclusive practices. We acknowledge that this shift in curation represents the passing of authority and power from the institution to the community. At conferences, we debate the relevance and the safety of self-curation and community curation. In fact, we often scoff at the idea of individuals/communities attempting to self-curate. It simply does not appear to be as authoritative as the curation that a museum professional could provide. After all, if people and communities could self-curate, why would museums need us? When asked this question, I always refer to my background as a librarian and answer, "People can get any book online these days, Google any term, learn anything on the Internet—they don't even need printed books . . . but do you see libraries going away? Do you see librarians disappearing from our society? NO. And do you know why? Because librarians realized what it was their community needed from them—they became relevant, and libraries have stayed important to society. We need to take a page from the book of librarians and learn what our communities need from us." Quite honestly, I've received a spectrum of feedback concerning this answer: from "yes, we should do that" to "I don't want to be a librarian. . . . I'm a _____." Yes, applying inclusion theory to your museum will require that you relinquish some of your authority over the collection, the exhibits, and even the narrative. (I will discuss this subject more in the disadvantages section of this chapter.) For now, however, imagine the powerful part your museum could play within your community just by framing difficult discussions within inclusion theory.

What about multiculturalism? First of all, the 1980s called: they want their theoretical framework back! Yes, multiculturalism is no longer in vogue at museum conferences. But, despite the changing trends in conferences, multiculturalism still governs modern museum exhibits and programming. In other words, if you looked closely at the practices of your institution, I suspect that you would find that multiculturalism is still at work—invisible, but influential. What is the problem with multiculturalism? Other than being outdated, how is this a bad thing? Multiculturalism invariably leads to thematically organized content: collections/exhibits/programming that centers around an idea designed by the museum professional. I have attended museum programming on folk dance in which various dance groups and organizations were carefully selected, lined up in order, paired off as one would pair wine and cheese, and paraded around the museum's rotunda. Is this an expression of culture? Or a curation of cultures? To understand the fallacy of multiculturalism, we must acknowledge that we anchored the concept to the museum professional's understanding of a culture or community. All too often we fail to realize that we are merely the keepers of the culture, not the congregation of the culture. What right do we have to curate culture for our communities?

Advantage 3: The Promotion of Museum Professionals as Cultural Facilitators

Inclusion theory, by contrast, allows museum professionals to serve as facilitators of culture. We act as the mediators between the museum space, objects, and community will. As museum professionals, this is not a natural role for some of us to step into, but I encourage you to try. Look at the example of the Wing Luke Museum of the Asian Pacific American Experience in Seattle, Washington. "The Wing," as it is informally known, is featured prominently in this book and is the focus of chapter 5. Of importance is that the museum professionals at "The Wing" do not see themselves in traditional museum roles such as "curators," "registrars," and "exhibit designers" (Coleman 2016b). They are part of their community. In fact, "The Wing" has functioned successfully for several decades through a model developed by the museum itself (Chinn 2006a). The Community-Based Exhibition Model asserts the significance of social relationships between the museum and the community (Chinn "About Us"; Chinn 2006a; Chinn 2016). I encourage you to research for yourself the powerful exhibits co-created by The Wing and its surrounding communities.

Advantage 4: The Awareness of Marginalization and Exclusion in Society

Inclusion generates awareness concerning marginalization and exclusion within society. A museum using inclusion theory as a framework for discussing exclusion will encounter hard truths about the community in which their museum resides. Why? Remember that social inclusion is a theory birthed from the presence of social exclusion, and it inherently directs the attention of citizens to the societal problems at hand (Rawal 2008). We cannot possibly expect museums to be agents of social change or justice if we cannot adopt an inclusive framework for our dialogues and practices (Coleman 2015). Although this advantage may appear to be little more than rhetoric, it has provoked much research throughout Western Europe and the United Kingdom, and we should not discount it. In museum research, there is the opportunity through social inclusion theory to realize that "contrary to conventional museum wisdom and discipline-based dogma, research and social action are not incompatible but are necessary allies" (Janes 2009). When museums employ inclusive practices, they will see marginalization within their community brought to light. Yes, inclusion is significant—it will impact your museum's ability to illuminate social injustice.

Advantage 5: The Reassurance of a Solution

At a foundational level, inclusion positively reassures society of two key assertions: yes, there is a problem; and yes, there is a solution. For instance, you may notice that your museum visitors appear to be predominantly Caucasian and that the only people of color in your museum are the custodial staff. You have realized that a real problem exists. And, as a real problem, it has a real solution. What is that solution? We will get to that. For now, know that each museum is unique, each exclusionary practice is unique, and every solution, while inclusive, is also unique. In using inclusion theory, we will gain the understanding that there

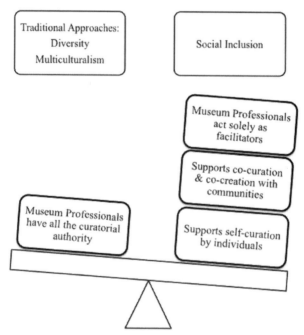

Figure 3.1.   Traditional Approaches versus Social Inclusion.
Created by Laura-Edythe Coleman.

is no one solution to societal problems of marginalization and division (Dodd et al. 2002; Dodd and Sandell 2001; Sandell 1998a, 401–18). A key advantage of inclusion theory is that because it is deeply rooted in the complex problems of real society, it also can help us look for multifaceted solutions. We will not fix exclusion solely by tackling a single facet. Why? Because cultural, social, political, and economic problems are inherently linked. At some point, every social problem is codependent on another—inclusion theory affirms this idea.

Disadvantages of Inclusion for Museums

Are there disadvantages to inclusion? Certainly, inclusion has some limitations. I outline these problems because I want museum professionals to be knowledgeable about the many facets of inclusion theory. A text on inclusion would be incomplete without explaining the possible disadvantages of inclusion. The first disadvantage is the infancy of inclusion terminology. It is nearly impossible for museum practitioners, researchers, and theorists to work with inclusion because we do not have an established shared vocabulary for doing so. Although I mentioned this problem earlier in chapter 2, it merits further explanation here. As a field, we have had little to no development of the terminology used by practitioners to articulate the social role of museums. In contrast, it is interesting to note that we do have decades of research into the formation of vocabulary for object-related museum work. For instance, we have numerous texts on classification schema for everything from plant species to works of art. Our predecessors in the field of museology have labored to create the language that we collectively use to describe exhibits, objects, conservation, and preservation. Only recently have we begun to move from object-oriented museology to people-oriented museology—a phenomenon that harkens back to the words of Stephen Weil that museums are transforming "from being about something to being for somebody" (Weil 2002). As we begin our discussions on the new social role of museums, we must also embark on the creation of a new layer of museum vocabulary: terminology that describes the social work of museums (Silverman 2010). The words that we choose now, as a field, to describe the inclusive museum will have a power that resonates for several generations of museum practice.

Disadvantage 1: The Infancy of Terminology

I note this infancy of terminology as a disadvantage in the use of inclusion theory. However, I would suggest that this limitation is also a unique strength: underdeveloped inclusion language may offer researchers and practitioners the chance to work together to craft a standard vocabulary. Rarely do we have the opportunity to impact the future of our field. And while we may be tempted to shy away from inclusion theory because of the lack of vocabulary, we should not. Instead, I encourage you to seize this moment and begin talking about inclusion. Who knows? You may create the next famous phrase! As you progress in your understanding of inclusion, try to remain inquisitive: always start conversations about inclusion by asking your fellow museum practitioners for their definition of inclusion. Begin each dialogue with an agreed-upon point concerning inclusion, and your conversation will be more fruitful (see figure 3.2 for words I have heard used to define inclusion). I suspect that if you follow my advice, you will soon discover a broad spectrum of thought on the subject of inclusion for museums. For instance, some of your colleagues will define inclusion in relation to diversity or accessibility, while others will link the concept to the problem of exclusion. Be advised that personal definitions of inclusion will differ from institutional ones; to quote many a museum practitioner's Twitter account, "Views do not reflect those of my museum." The disconnect between individuals and institutional definitions of inclusion may reflect several positions. On the one hand, you may encounter an individual who feels passionately committed to changing exclusive practices into inclusive ones and impacting their community through their museum. Such individuals often approach me at conferences, troubled by the "cold" stance

attachment
acceptance
rapport
community
loyalty friendship
inclusion
welcome
belonging
kinship
affinity
association

Figure 3.2.   Inclusion Terminologies.
Created by Laura-Edythe Coleman.

of their institutions to serve objects over people. On the other hand, you may meet individuals who believe that the care of objects suffers and that the narrative is inaccurate when curated inclusively with their communities. These practitioners approach me at conferences and often express that they feel burdened by the demands of their progressive museum board to be more inclusive. I cannot ignore the disconnect between individual museum practitioners and their institutions, and this gulf should no longer be neglected. Be prepared for the definitions, terminology, and dialogues to be difficult—at least at first. As you encounter this first disadvantage of inclusion theory, recognize that this is also a unique opportunity to craft our professional language.

Disadvantage 2: We Need More Research

Another disadvantage to inclusion theory is that it has been researched very little within the United States—especially as it relates to museum applications. Such is not the case in the United Kingdom, where social inclusion theory (note the combined term *social inclusion*) has been heavily researched for several decades (Sandell 1998, 401–18; Dodd et al. 2002; Dodd and Sandell 2001).

The ambiguous nature of social inclusion theory terminology is found throughout the layers of British society, including the many levels of museum professionals (Tlili 2008, 123–47). Tlili conducted a series of interviews with museum professionals at four UK institutions. A cross section of the staff was interviewed concerning their own perceptions of social inclusion and the role of museums in social inclusion. Tlili determined that within those four UK museums, "Social inclusion has redefined the organizational priorities and the organizational identity of the museum, thus causing a ripple effect on the professional cultures and identities within the museum, and the balance of power between these" (Tlili 2008, 142). According to Tlili's findings, social inclusion can have impressive impact on institutional priorities. Are we, as American museum professionals, not seeking a way to transform museum practice?

Tlili carefully interviewed museum personnel, gaining multiple perspectives. In doing so, his work illuminated the organizational divisions within the museum. His particular approach quickly revealed the ambiguity of the term *social inclusion*. Tlili refers to social inclusion as both "generic" and complex, as it is an "object of struggle as it lends itself to multiple and conflicting social ontologies and causal explanations" (Tlili 2008, 123–24). In his interviews of museum curators concerning their definitions of social inclusion, they predominantly referred to social inclusion as an accessibility issue. Curator interpretation of social inclusion policy centered on making the museum accessible to marginalized community groups. Upon deeper examination, it became apparent that under the New Labour government in the United Kingdom, making the museum accessible was necessary to increase museum attendance among underrepresented groups. Under New Labour, museums became government funded, and entrance fees per visitor were no longer collected. In turn, museums were expected to increase museum attendance in a way that would reflect the demographics of the entire population of Britain. For the museum professionals interviewed by Tlili, social inclusion was no longer a concept concerning broad social change but also a label for museum attendance quotas.

Tlili's research revealed that social inclusion theory has unintended consequences on policy and, in turn, an impact on museum professional identity. Museum professionals interviewed by Tlili (2008) discussed their role in social inclusion in terms of numerical increases of marginalized community attendees. Tlili contends that museum professionals have changed the nature of social inclusion in museums such that "the organizational 'construct' of social inclusion is to a great extent governed by a numerical logic" (Tlili 2008, 143). Museum professionals reported a perceived threat to their professional identity due to the emphasis placed by policymakers on proving the numerical changes. Tlili proposes that the strength that social inclusion theory adds to museums is, to some degree, countered by the weakness introduced to museum professional identity.

This weakness has been noted in a number of studies in which museum professionals struggled to define the term *social inclusion*. The 2000 GLLAM report, a production of the Research Centre for Museums and Galleries at the University of Leicester, reflected exploratory research within twenty-two museums across the United Kingdom. The Group for Large Local Authority Museums (GLLAM) research faced difficulties due to the various definitions of social inclusion, a term that the researchers deemed "fuzzy" (Group for Large Local Authority Museums 2000, 1–59). In fact, many UK researchers and museum professionals are hesitant to explicitly define *inclusion*. I believe that we do not need to maintain this level of ambiguity in our vocabulary. In fact, it is imperative that our field defines the term *inclusion* now.

American museum professionals need answers that only research upon American institutions will provide. Although American and UK museums are similar and arguably share a certain lineage, the differences between the two are significant. We can, of course, learn from the more than twenty years of research performed in the United Kingdom, but we need scientific research that accounts for the differences between American museums and UK institutions. Research must be conducted that accounts for the fact that inclusion is not mandated in the

United States as it is in the United Kingdom. The demographics between the two nations are also different, the forms of exclusion occurring in each nation are disparate, and this will surely impact US museums' ability to combat social exclusion. I propose that such research be undertaken in partnership between American and UK researchers. As a field, we will not understand inclusion in America until proper scientific research is conducted, preferably longitudinal studies. In particular, we should investigate the variations of language surrounding the term *inclusion* throughout the world, and study the ambiguity of the language in diverse communities.

Disadvantage 3: Ambiguity of Language

The ambiguity of social inclusion theory extends beyond terminology to scope of application. Until recently, social inclusion theory has been focused on application to the economic and political aspects of exclusion. Historically, research into social inclusion theory articulates an acknowledgment of cultural dimensions of exclusion without addressing the solutions to cultural exclusion. Social inclusion theory may be refined through research to become more balanced in its approach to the multiple dimensions of exclusion. An important outcome of refining social inclusion theory should be the ability to account more accurately for the cultural needs of those being marginalized.

A standardized social inclusion vocabulary is an important step in the production of valuable museum assessment tools. The demands of policymakers to produce measurable social change may be countered by industry definitions of inclusion and museum professional associations. As I will discuss in chapter 5, the first step for successful inclusion assessment involves vocabulary development. Although social inclusion theory has influenced both museum research and practice, the evaluation of museum impact upon marginalized groups has only just begun. Lynda Kelly notes in her Australian-based museum research that "there is no one template for measuring museum impact, no one set of indicators, and no precise path for mapping the relationship between museums and individuals/communities" (Kelly 2006). Researchers attempting museum impact evaluation generally agree that such assessments should connect back to the communities involved: the long-term impact of museums should be considered not only at the level of the visitor but also at the level of the communities that museums serve. Thus, understanding the long-term impact of museums enables a better understanding of how to serve and enrich communities, of which museums are a part (Kelly 2005, 45–69; Kelly 2006; Falk 1992; Falk, Heimlich, and Bronnenkant 2008, 55–79; Falk 2009; Falk et al. 2010, 249–58).

Disadvantage 4: Unknown and Unmeasured

The socially inclusive role of the museum is unknown and unmeasured, despite the assumption that museums can and are acting as agents of social change. Sandell has asked, "If museums contribute toward the exclusion of groups and individuals from society, might they also possess the capability to help retrieve and re-integrate those excluded?" (Sandell 1998, 408). Museums wield tremendous power to change society, to uphold society, and to affirm society. Social inclusion advocates that everyone should have access to and be represented by museums, thus limiting the marginalization of particular groups. A question remains unanswered: To what degree, if any, does social inclusion theory influence museum policy, practice, and impact?

In the example of Lynda Kelly's research on social inclusion in Australian museums, policymakers have recognized the significance of social inclusion theory application for use in museum societal impact measurement. Kelly reports, "Museums Archives Libraries Council has taken a leading role in areas of social inclusion and measuring learning and impact across the cultural sector in the United Kingdom, which has provided a useful template for others to adapt and learn from" (Kelly 2006, 68). As we implement social inclusion theory in museum policy, practice, and evaluation, it will be even more necessary to publicize the social purpose of museums lest the work become invisible.

The Duality of Inclusion

An important aspect of inclusion theory is the duality of the concept. (Social) inclusion aligns well philosophically with theories of the social construction of reality (Silver 1994, 531). Berger and Luckmann propose that reality is co-constructed by individuals in context or situation (Berger 1990). From this perspective, knowledge and identity cannot be generated in a context void of society (Sutton 1993, 411–30). Social inclusion emphasizes that society has a role in both problems of exclusivity and inclusive solutions. Regardless of the museum exhibit content or the divisions within society, social inclusion theory focuses our attention holistically on the multiple agents and forces at work within the museum experience.

Inclusion Theory Has Potential

Inclusion theory has incredible potential to reveal the problems within both our museums and our society. A primary advantage of inclusion is that it expands the social role of the museum—a task that has been assigned to the American museum field for several decades. Museum professionals can adapt inclusion theory to be a framework for dialogue between stakeholders and a starting point for community self-curation. As museum professionals grow into the new role of cultural facilitators, they can leverage inclusion theory to expand debates beyond the traditional discourse of diversity and multiculturalism. The duality of inclusion offers a level of theoretical flexibility never before seen in our field. Aided by inclusion theory, museum professionals can be reassured that their museum will illuminate exclusion and develop lasting solutions to problems of marginalization and discrimination. In the next chapter, we will explore the various tools for implementing inclusion practices in your museum.

4

Creating Cultural Inclusion

Partnerships with People

Inclusion is a spectrum on which any museum may exist. American museums are only now becoming aware of the notion of inclusivity. The vast majority of American museums are along the lower end of the inclusivity spectrum: the first-tier "inclusive" museum. As museums progress along the spectrum of inclusivity, their impacts become greater upon society. It is natural that museums should begin at the starting point of this spectrum, on the individual level: the museum visitor. After all, human society is composed of individuals, and museums can embark on an inclusive agenda simply by changing how they interact with individuals. In this chapter, I will focus almost exclusively on the relationship a museum may have with an individual. In order for museums to cultivate relationships with the individual visitors, we must focus on particular components of this relationship. Partnerships with people are threefold: *personal*, *participatory*, and *portable* (see figure 4.1). In exploring these three components, we will learn to improve upon them and why it is vital to make these connections with our visitors now.

Personal

The museum must learn to make partnerships with individuals—not just stereotypes or archetypes. There are several key

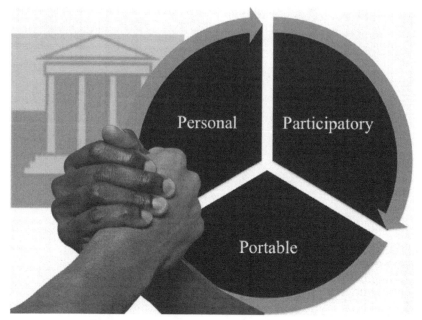

Figure 4.1.   Attributes of Tier 1 Inclusion: Partnerships with People.
Created by Laura-Edythe Coleman.

elements to forming relationships with individuals. First, museums must recognize that people arrive at the museum with their own lived experiences. We often have the misconception that the people who visit our museums come to our exhibits with certain knowledge (or lack thereof). Indeed, art museums are known for expecting, if subtly so, a level of sophisticated knowledge from their visitors. Science and history museums tend to assume their visitors have little prior subject knowledge, or have incorrect knowledge. Neither of these approaches is quite right. Individual visitors have personal histories, and sometimes personal relationships, with the history, art, or science that the museum presents. Assuming that museum visitors all have equitable knowledge concerning subjects will set up your exhibits for failure. There are multiple sources to describe the role that prior experience plays in the museum visit (Falk 2000; Falk and Dierking 1992; Falk, Heimlich, and Bronnenkant 2008, 55–79; Falk et al. 2010, 249–58; Serrell 1996). We must respect our visitors by honoring their prior knowledge. All too often, we believe, misguidedly, that our museum visitors are empty vessels and, as such, are waiting for the carefully curated knowledge presented in our exhibits. In general, as a museum professional, we must take care not to assume anything about our visitors: that they have expert knowledge or none at all. There is also the antithesis of this scenario: the overzealous education program. Remember that education is not about testing, nor should your museum exhibits be created in such a way as to be "tests" of the visitors' knowledge or experiences. All too often, museum professionals want to know whether the visitors learned the educational takeaway from an exhibit. The museum experience is not about their knowledge; it is not about whether you as the museum professional did your job correctly in telling a story or narrative. It is about the interpersonal co-construction of individualized meaning for the museum visitor. In other words, it's not about you.

Second, as in library science, we must provide entry points to the collection and the narrative for all visitors. We understand that if we do not offer these entry points or wayfinding tools, our visitors will have a personal experience with the museum similar to that of Michelle Obama. As mentioned in chapter 1, the former First Lady could not see herself in the standard museum collection or exhibit and therefore found no entry point into the narrative (Chasmer 2015). If we are to succeed in making our museums personal, we must provide pathways for all people.

Third, we must provide equitable service, on an individual level, to our visitors. Not every visitor will need assistance to attend the museum, but some will require great attention. As a public institution, you will have individuals from all walks of life—and some of those individuals will be experiencing social exclusion, as I have already discussed, based upon one or more of these dimensions: cultural, economic, social, or political. Museums must make an effort to provide equitable assistance to those less able to attend and participate. To see some ways of doing this, let's take a page out of library history: Keep the museum open later or earlier. As a result, your institution may close one extra day per week. However, you must provide ways for those who work long shifts to attend your museum. Are you charging admission, perhaps because you have no choice? Look for inventive ways to provide memberships—the Chicago public library system has teamed up with local museums and zoos to deliver memberships that can be "checked out" for a day by families (see figure 4.2). In this way, library patrons who pay nothing for

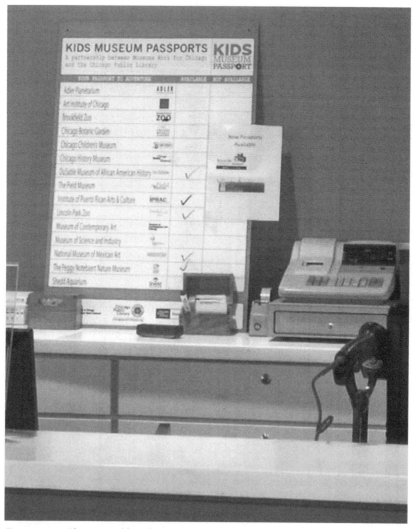

Figure 4.2. Chicago Public Library Museum Pass Program.
Created by Laura-Edythe Coleman.

library services can obtain a day pass for their family to attend a museum or zoo that might otherwise have been cost prohibitive.

Consider holding free events, or finding funding that can subsidize the cost being covered by museum admissions tickets. Is just getting there an obstacle for individuals in your community? Some may have a car, while others may ride a bus or public transport, but what about those individuals who live in rural communities? Rural communities account for 97 percent of American land and 19.3 percent of the total US population, roughly sixty million individuals nationwide (Bureau). For Americans residing in rural communities with little or no access to cultural institutions such as museums, the public library system acts as a lifeline to those in need (Griffiths and King 2008). Across all of America, 67 percent of all individuals age sixteen years and older stated that if their local public library closed, it would affect their families personally (Griffiths and King 2008). Do we believe that Americans would declare the same for their local museums? Do Americans believe that if their local museum were to close, this loss would impact their families personally? I do not believe that American museums have, as a whole, attempted to personalize the experience for their visitors. We need to begin to tailor our work to the individual, not just to the broader community. I will cover partnerships with other community programs in chapter 5, but start thinking now about how you can reach individuals through already established pathways such as libraries. You may not need to create an entirely new road; you can start driving on an existing one as long as you continue to meet the individual needs of your museum visitors.

Participatory

If you are only now hearing about the participatory museum, please visit Nina Simon's website (http://www.participatory museum.org/) and read her online copy of the book by the same name, *The Participatory Museum*. Nina Simon promotes a "well-scaffolded participatory experience" for museums (Simon 2010). In her successful model of participation, Simon advocates "two counter-intuitive design principles": first, museum visitors "thrive on constraints"; and second, visitor engagement must be "personal, not social" (Simon 2010). Without fail, when these two principles are enacted they will illicit participation successfully. According to Simon, "Meaningful constraints motivate and focus participation" (Simon 2010). But how and why do limitations help museum visitors to participate? Constraints break larger, seemingly impossible tasks into smaller ones for visitors to more easily complete. Instead of asking museum visitors to produce new works of art, museum educators have begun to carefully construct experiences in which individuals may contribute and collaborate in the creation of exhibits. This approach is not new to educational pedagogy; teachers have often divided complex problems into a series of simple steps. Art museum educators have long thought that museum visitors wanted a blank canvas and the opportunity to create. Simon argues differently that the "materials are not the barriers—the ideas and the confidence are" (Simon 2010). Museums have followed this shift in participation engagement techniques, either intuitively or by reading Simon's work. Successful participatory exhibits provide simple instructions and clear constraints for the museum visitor to work within.

The second principle, "personal, not social," is best seen in participatory exhibits that speak to individual museum visitors. This concept may seem oversimplified, but museum professionals often envision museum visitors as an amalgamated population—a segment of society. True participatory exhibits speak to the unique visitor. In the 9/11 Memorial Museum in New York City, museum visitors are encouraged to write a message about their experience upon an ever-changing, ephemeral wall (see figure 4.3). This installation won the 2015 American Alliance of Museums (AAM) Silver Muse Award for Interactive Kiosks. The installation, *Signing Steel Interactive*, was described by AAM Muse judges as follows:

> This is a well thought out and executed example of creating a community in the way it ties a digital remembrance book to people and place. Also impressive was the immediacy of the interactive with the geolocated signature appearing just seconds after it is written, allowing people to share their personal testimony and story right there, right then. This is an

interactive that is simple, emotionally connected, beautiful and socially engaging. (American Alliance of Museums 2015)

As a participatory experience, this installation allows visitors to express their voice and to dialogue with others in a space of extreme significance.

In the Wing Luke Museum, featured in the next chapter, each exhibit has an element that elicits a response from museum visitors, a "ritual act," as one curator described (Coleman 2016b). Examples of inclusive, participatory acts within the exhibits are: museum visitors are encouraged to "pay tribute and lighting [*sic*] a candle—so we use the battery operated lights so that people are able to place something"; museum visitors leave their message in exhibits by a "Shinto tradition of writing a message and then tying it" (Coleman 2016b). Ultimately, the Wing Luke Museum staff indicated that these ritual acts and the Community-Based Exhibition Model empowered local communities to tell their stories, combining inclusion and identity work in an authentic space:

> To make our exhibits more inclusive, we include more inter-actives so visitors can contribute to our exhibition—so, they might be prompted with a question. In *Bojagi* (a recent exhibit)

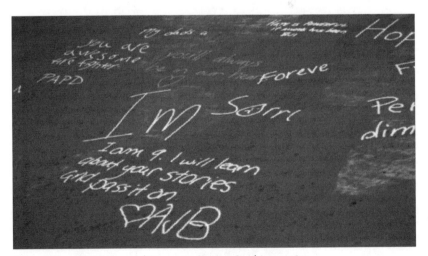

Figure 4.3. *9/11 Memorial Museum,* Signing Steel Interactive.
Coleman 2016a and 2016b.

"Our Neighborhood is Our Largest Exhibition"

Figure 4.4.   The Wing Luke Museum of the Asian Pacific American Experience.
Coleman 2016a and 2016b.

> at the end of the exhibit there's several questions like "what informs your identity?" "What do you want your legacy to be?" So it doesn't have to be ethnic-specific—it's for everyone. So they become a part of the exhibit. (Coleman 2016b)

Participatory museums are formed to incorporate individuals into the exhibit through individual interactions. This is not a new trend, but it is recent enough in museology memory to merit more study. There is plenty of evidence to show that participatory equals memorable experiences. The Wing Luke Museum is integrated into its neighborhood so fully that the director, Beth Takekawa, has been known to say, "Our neighborhood is our largest exhibition" (Coleman 2016b). The Wing Luke Museum has leveraged participatory experiences so greatly that the institution is incorporated into community memory (see figure 4.4).

Portable

To make museums truly inclusive, we must make our exhibits more than just personal and participatory for the individual but also portable. The average museum visitor should be able to walk away from your museum with a new element woven into their identity. I am not saying that your exhibits will transform every museum visitor—this seems a lofty goal, to say the least—but we should aim for this result. Because when we generate personal and participatory experiences that transform individuals, those visitors will carry the museum exhibit out the door with them. We should make it our goal to have exhibits that promote the extension of museum content beyond the thresholds of our doors. Bewildered museum professionals often greet me at conferences and demand to know, "How are we supposed to reach our entire community? We could never manage that!" And the truth is: no, you cannot do that on your own. But what you can do is enlist the average museum visitor in a strategy to reach everyone in your community. How? There are many levels of activating your museum visitors to be agents of inclusion. These efforts range from highly visible programs to subtle forms of exhibit portability. Remember: your exhibits are not necessarily what must be portable; the museum itself is a fixed place. People are never still; we move constantly. We need to leverage the portability of visitors—they are part of your museum. Have you ever considered your visitors to be a part of your museum? (See figure 4.5.) We tend to consider museum visitors as external stakeholders, but what if they are not? What if museum visitors are part of the content? The programming? The exhibits? Why are we determined to limit the virtually limitless abilities of those who live near our museums? If this describes your museum, and perhaps the viewpoints of museum professionals in general, I believe it is time to change. More and more often museums are becoming experiential, digital, ethereal, and the only constants in the museum equation are the people who will visit them. I urge you and your museum to take steps now to envision the role of museum visitors differently—in activating these individuals in *personal*, *participatory*, and *portable* ways, you will become the first tier of the inclusive museum.

How can we make museums more portable? The United States Holocaust Memorial Museum (USHMM) recently celebrated twenty years of its individualized portable program *Bringing*

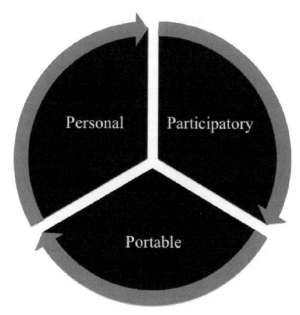

Figure 4.5.   Partnerships with People.
Coleman 2016.

the Lessons Home. In this student program, the USHMM activates individual high school students to become ambassadors of the museum to their families and communities. Through the USHMM, *"Bringing the Lessons Home* program introduces thousands of Washington, DC, area high school students to Holocaust history each year. The program also enables the most inspired of those students to become tour guides and ambassadors through their high school years and beyond. These ambassadors then share the history and its relevance with their families, friends, and communities." Evaluation of this program revealed the "emergence of a model that conveys the system of complex relationships between personal growth and individual outcomes and community actions and public value outcomes. . . . Each role provided a bridge that eventually connected the learning of individual programme participants to changes in larger communities" (Scott 2013).

The USHMM *Bringing the Lessons Home* program took time and effort to craft, but ultimately it has proven successful for twenty years.

About Accessibility

Museums need to be accessible to all people. Period. Yet many museums are not yet accessible to everyone. Art museums, while beginning to adopt transformative ways of displaying art for the blind, are still behind (Wecker 2015). Many museums reside in historic buildings, and due to architectural concerns they cannot be modified to be handicap accessible. I believe that museums should be accessible for all and inclusive of everyone. A primary mistake made by museums and museum professionals is equating accessibility with inclusion. In recent years, accessibility has been the substitute for inclusive practice. Accessibility is not inclusion.

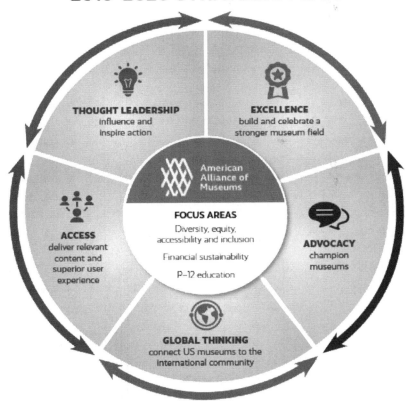

Figure 4.6. AAM Strategic Plan.
American Alliance of Museums, "Strategic Plan."

If by all measures a museum is inclusive, it will naturally also be accessible. The inverse is not true, that an accessible museum is an inclusive one. In fact, these two ideas are not even on the same conceptual level. Why do we often hear these words together? Basically, we have a common misunderstanding of these concepts. In figure 4.6, note the combined role of diversity, equity, accessibility, and inclusion emphasized by the strategic plan of the American Alliance of Museums (American Alliance of Museums "Strategic Plan"). Please do not misunderstand my perspective here—museums should be accessible, must be accessible, yet being so does not mean they are automatically inclusive institutions.

Proposed Evaluation Techniques for Tier 1 Inclusive Museums

The traditional quantitative techniques such as visitor surveying and exhibition studies work well for analyzing the inclusivity of a tier 1 inclusive museum. What should you be looking for in an evaluation of a tier 1 museum? When I examine a tier 1 inclusive museum, I examine instances in which curatorial voice is shared between the museum and the visitor; representations of those individuals traditionally marginalized within exhibits; and presentations of contested histories or issues. I collect quantitative data such as demographics, attendance numbers, and collection metadata. I also rely on qualitative techniques such as interviewing and ethnographic studies. I examine qualitatively the perceptions of museum visitors and staff concerning exhibits, collections, community issues, and the role of the museum. I outline my favorite quantitative and qualitative techniques in chapter 8 (see also figure 4.7).

Inclusion Is a Journey

In 2000, the UK Department for Culture, Media, and Sport outlined the "basic components of an evolving social inclusion

Proposed Evaluation
Techniques for Tier 1
Inclusive Museums

Quantitative
- Visitor Surveys
- Collection & Exhibit Studies

Qualitative
- Interviews
- Focus Groups
- Ethnographic Studies

Figure 4.7.   Proposed Evaluation Techniques of Tier 1 Inclusion.
Created by Laura-Edythe Coleman.

policy for publicly funded museums, galleries and archives"
(DCMS 2000, 1–36). In this document, UK policymakers ac-
knowledged a "First Stage: Access—becoming inclusive and
accessible organisations" (DCMS 2000, 1–36). This primary stage
is one of three in a greater framework for a "journey towards social inclusion (that) will have a number of stages" (DCMS 2000,
1–36). I encourage you and your museum to begin at once on
this primary level of inclusivity, engaging the singular museum
visitor and attempting to mitigate social exclusion on the individual level. As Chris Cardiel, from the Oregon Museum of Science and Industry, stated, "A member of an under-represented
group should not feel they are the only ones advocating for inclusion and diversity . . . that should be everyone's responsibility" (Cardiel and Borland 2015). If we truly believe that inclusion
is our responsibility, then we should act decisively to cultivate a
culture of inclusion for every individual museum visitor. In the
next chapter, we will discuss the secondary level of inclusivity
for your museum: partnerships with programs.

5

Aiding in Social Regeneration

Partnerships with Programs, Agencies, and Community Organizations

No museum is an island unto itself. Instead, each museum is an oasis of culture for our society and an integral thread in the fabric of a community. The ideas presented in this chapter are far from new but rarely adopted. In 1999, Stephen Weil of the Smithsonian delivered a message to the British Museum Annual Meeting:

> As the museum redefines its central purpose from inward to outward—from amassing a collection to providing a public service—it finds itself being drawn into collaboration with, or at times even exchanging functions with, a broad range of other community-based service organizations whose purposes are similar. (Weil 1999)

In the almost two decades since Weil's words, little has been done by the American museum field to realize this vision. The time has come for American museums to partner with community programs for the benefit of society. In this chapter I outline the second tier of the inclusive museum—*aiding in social regeneration: partnerships with programs, agencies, and community organization* (Sandell 1998, 401–18; DCMS 2000, 1–36). For many museum professionals, the prospect of community partnerships is unnerving at best and unwelcome at worst. In this chapter, I will explore why there are hindrances to partnerships with

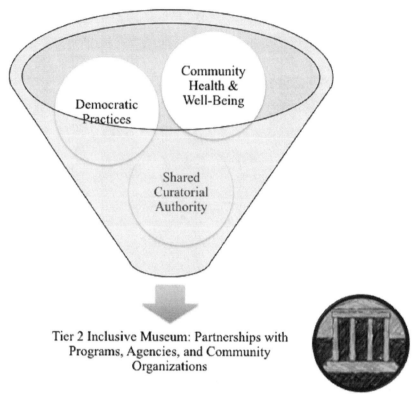

Figure 5.1. Attributes of a Tier 2 Inclusive Museum.
Created by Laura-Edythe Coleman.

community organizations. I will also outline how we can transform our perspectives while still staying true to our mission statements, and I will provide examples of successful museum–community agency partnerships.

Hindrances

Institutional Identity

Imagine for a moment that your museum had no mission statement. You are a building filled with a collection and educated professionals. Who are you to your community? What is your museum to your community? At one point in your institution's history, your mission was to collect and catalog items. Soon after, your museum began to display and exhibit objects. Naturally, you started to preserve and protect your collection for future generations. Museum professionals, isolated from society, did their work, and these were not activities that required a partnership with other organizations. The curator's job has been historically a solo endeavor. Museums, like the curators who work within them, have become solitary organizations. Do places truly take on the personality of their inhabitants? I think so, and museums are no different. Museums are highly specialized spaces, crafted by specialists. As American museums are evolving, their identity within society is also emerging to be different. For many in the museum field, the blurring of institutional identity is disturbing. We should not fear this change, for "whatever loss that might entail, however, may be more than compensated for by the increase in effectiveness it can thereby achieve" (Weil 1999).

The Physicality of the Museum

Museums are to protect objects, and therefore collections must be physically separated from society. People, as physical beings, naturally erode the surfaces they touch. As museum professionals, we value the role of physical barriers—for example, glass protects items from wear; gloves keep our hands from disturbing parchment. We must keep many of the items that we curate in climate-controlled environments—humidity and temperature monitored continuously. The isolation of museum objects behind glass and on display has resulted in the well-documented phenomenon known as the *museum effect* (Alpers in Karp and Lavine 1991). The museum effect is "the tendency to isolate something from its world, to offer it up for attentive looking and thus to transform it into art like our own" (Alpers in Karp and Lavine 1991). How does the preservation of items relate to an institution's partnership with community agencies? Quite simply, not only do these physical barriers keep our objects safe, but they also keep these objects from people. These physical dividers lead to a striking difference in our ability to relate to other nonprofit organizations that are in constant contact with people. This may not seem like a vast difference, but I believe that we inherently sense this division, and others in our community do as well.

Museums Have Specific Missions and Cannot Afford Mission Creep

American museum professionals recognize that their institutions have specific mission and vision statements. As professionals, it is important to acknowledge that these mission statements are the guiding documents of our museums. In recent years serious criticism of museum–community program partnerships has arisen due to the possible risk of mission creep: the undesirable gradual change of an institution's objectives. Critics such as Chet Orloff, manager of the Pamplin International Collection of Art & History, stated that museums that alter their traditional missions to become "social justice agencies" would be participating in "a risky business that may win some short term gains but results in the diminution of other vital services they provide their communities" (Orloff 2017, 33–36). I respectfully disagree with such criticism, as did Stephen Weil, as these partnerships are more costly in the short term and provide long-term benefits to both the museum and the community (Weil 1999).

Curatorial Authority Is Threatened by Lowering Barriers

Museum professionals enjoy a sacred status within our society. Society trusts our museums above many other sources available to provide accurate information (Griffiths and King 2008). We value that status. Museum professionals, especially curators, do not enjoy the feeling of "surrender" as they allow external consultants to craft text and arrange displays (Scott 2013, 101). For many museum professionals, allowing others to craft our narratives is tantamount to abandoning historical or scientific accuracy. Despite that fear, when those narratives are crafted by input from the community, the curatorial voices of all are clearly heard.

Transformation Processes

Is it really as simple as Dana wrote, to "learn what aid the community needs . . . fit the museum to those needs" (Weil 1999)? It must be more difficult or complicated than what Dana suggests, or every museum would be undergoing a transformation process to become a strong partner with their communities. I propose a rethinking of these transformations: instead of difficult, let us consider the task of partnership as requiring an effort worthy of the rewards, and not necessarily complicated but nuanced to meet the unique needs of both the community and the museum. Perhaps this thinking is naïve—but not impossible. As we will see in the following examples, museum–community program partnerships are worthwhile, and the transformational processes to create those partnerships have several integral components: *relationships are valued more than results; time is at the disposal of all; democracy is practiced; the health and well-being of the community comes first.*

Relationships Are Valued More Than Results

In the successful museum–community partnerships we will explore, the museum professionals prioritize relationships (Coleman 2016b; Chinn 2006b). A successful exhibition for a museum is often measured in daily attendance, increasing memberships, and participation in educational programming. These measures are useful, but they hardly grant a holistic view of the impact of the museum on the community. Museum educators attempt to measure knowledge acquired by individuals and school groups attending an exhibit with entrance and exit surveys. Such metrics reveal the recall and precision of student memories post-exhibit but in no way explore the significance of the exhibit upon those communities. In studying museum–community partnerships, I have found that museum professionals who emphasize the strength of their relationship with the community also can speak to the success of their exhibitions. In the case of the Wing Luke Museum, museum staffs work with the community through a Community Advisory Committee, or CAC (Chinn 2006a). Cassie

Chinn of the Wing Luke Museum describes her relationship with community members as being the significant outcome of the exhibition process, not the other way around (Chinn 2016). Instead of the exhibit being the outcome of the relationship, the Wing Luke staff view the relationship as a result. This notion flies in the face of more traditional thoughts of "value-added" in which the relationship that develops with the community is a perk to the more important purpose of designing an exhibition. Does your museum value the relationships with the community more than the outcomes of exhibit design? One of the first transformational processes that your museum can do is changing the way in which you think about value, impact, and *relationships*.

Time Is at the Disposal of All

As the song and psalm go, there is a time for everything, a season. The second component to the transformational process of museum–community program partnerships is a changed notion of time. Yes, we all have deadlines—but are these shared deadlines? We all understand that the timing of an exhibit is significant. Most often, we view the calendar of exhibit openings and programming as a function of efficiency. When can we open an exhibition and receive the most traffic? When can we offer a program so that it is visible to stakeholders and thus increase our revenue through donations? In studying successful museum–community program partnerships, I have discovered an alternative perspective for viewing time. Instead of looking for efficient times for exhibition, museum professionals can look for *agreeable moments to exhibit*. In other words, is this the right time to approach this topic in your community? Is your community ready to address this exhibit? Have you asked your community program partners whether this is the best occasion? Perhaps as curators, we have become accustomed to making all of these decisions on our own. I suggest that we work with our community partners to determine timing, be more flexible in our times, and be prepared to stop work entirely on a topic until the time is right.

Democracy Is Practiced

America is a democracy; yet most museums do not run on a democratic model. Instead, American museums have heavily developed their organizational model to be bureaucracies or businesses. Neither of these formats, bureaucracies or businesses, suits the needs of a strong museum–community program partnership, as authority is not shared evenly within these formats. For your museum to become more inclusive, it must become more democratic in its relationship with the community. One can hardly expect a museum to be inclusive if it does not practice inclusivity in the co-construction of collections and exhibits. In a culturally inclusive exhibition, different voices—even those traditionally marginalized—are heard. To create healthy museum–community program partnerships, *we must practice inclusion and democracy as a co-creative transformational process.*

The Health and Well-Being of the Community Comes First

Which comes first: your museum or your community? If you consider your museum already woven into the fabric of the community, it may be a great deal easier to commit to this transformational process. Yes, your museum must maintain visitor attendance figures, produce revenue, and provide educational programming. Do these outcomes put the health and well-being of your community first? Do any of your corporate sponsors impact your choices in exhibits? For example, if one of your donors is the local gas company, do you shy away from exhibit development around environmental issues? In another example, as the Japanese American community changed, so did the museum programming at the Japanese American National Museum (JANM). The JANM curators reported the recent example of an exhibit containing contested subject matter, *Perseverance* (Coleman 2016b). The show *Perseverance* focused upon tattoo culture and was "very controversial amongst the docent population" (Coleman 2016b). One curator noted that the older docents generally associated tattoos with illicit gang activity and that "the older generation are not as excited about tattoos as say the younger generation are" (Coleman 2016b). One curator described the contested work of JANM like this:

> I'm not sure what point this would be or what term, but one of the challenges of working with a community organization is that there's a lot of controversies within the community. How do you address both without taking sides? So any curators who were to come in would have to find a way to tell both stories in a way that doesn't feel like we're manipulating the story. (Coleman 2016b)

In successful museum–community program partnerships, the health and well-being of the community comes first.

Nestled in Seattle's Chinatown-International District is the Wing Luke Museum of the Asian Pacific American Experi-

Figure 5.2.   The Wing Luke Museum of the Asian Pacific American Experience.
Coleman 2016a and 2016b (based on "Letter Cloud" by Erin Shie Palmer, 2008).

ence. This community-based museum contains temporary and permanent exhibitions. The Wing Luke Museum offers guided tours of the museum and the adjoining preserved historic hotel, as well as walking tours throughout the international district. As a neighborhood museum, the *institutional identity* of the Wing Luke is not a hindrance but a benefit to community partnerships. The mission of the Wing Luke Museum is "To connect everyone to the rich history, dynamic cultures and art of the Asian Pacific Americans through vivid storytelling and inspiring experiences" (Chinn "About Us"). The Wing Luke Museum's mission specifically connects the museum to the community nearby, and the institution does not suffer from the *hindrance of mission creep.*

Unlike the traditional museum, the Wing Luke Museum has engaged in a Community-Based Exhibition Model (CBEM), a format that "builds upon a basic exhibition development model but strives to infuse community members throughout the entire process" (Chinn 2006a, 15) (see figure 5.3).

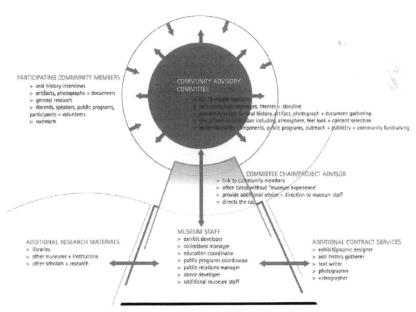

Figure 5.3. The Wing Luke Museum Community-Based Exhibit Model.

In short, the Wing Luke Museum is described like this:

Our institution is about people—the people whose stories are reflected in our walls, the people who work and volunteer throughout the year, the people who come to visit and experience, the people who came before us, and the people who have yet to come. (Chinn 2006a, 13)

The museum professionals at the Wing Luke Museum place relationship building above exhibition development in the museum's priorities: "The exhibition . . . is often times secondary to the primary goal which is the community building—the connections and the relationships" (Chinn 2006a, 13).

For every exhibit generated by the Wing Luke Museum, a Community Advisory Committee (CAC) is formed. A CAC is made up of community members with direct ties to the exhibit subject. The museum works with the CAC to determine subject matter and approach. The CAC develops exhibit messages and themes based on its members' perspectives and what they want visitors to learn about their community. The chosen subject matter may be highly contested, examine stereotypes, or explore difficult histories. One museum staff member described the subject matter chosen by CACs for exhibition like this: "We've had some very momentous events that have shaped the course of the way a community looks today—like the 1882 Chinese Exclusion Act—obviously the World War II Japanese American incarceration experience. So our job within that is to—in an on-going basis—share those stories and voices of the experiences of the past because that gives us root and understanding but also to share the voices of the present experience because that's who we are today and how people identify, and . . . then to continue to lay a place for those voices to continue to be heard—that's the future element!" (Coleman 2016b).

The Wing Luke Museum provides a space for difficult dialogues among the community, and the "museum continues to be an important place where the Asian Pacific American community looks to for engagement, inspiration and leadership" (Chinn "About Us").

In my studies of the Wing Luke Museum, interviewees described the *curatorial voice* at the Wing Luke Museum as the "authentic voice" of the communities involved. One interviewee spoke of the difference between the Wing Luke Museum and traditional museums thusly: "Here at the Wing Luke Museum then we both try to recognize and acknowledge that there's been that long-standing context for curatorial voice (in traditional museums). Questioning perhaps—whose voices haven't been heard in that context?" The Wing Luke Museum serves as a space devoted to "providing a place for more voices to be heard" (Coleman 2016b). For the Wing Luke Museum, *curatorial authority is not threatened* by community partnerships; instead, the Wing Luke curators share curatorial authority with their community counterparts.

In particular, the Wing Luke Community-Based Exhibition Model (CBEM) reflects the direct engagement of community members in formulating narratives (see appendix for complete details on the CBEM). As the community members create the exhibit text, they often generate labels that are in the first person. One curator reported, "A lot of times CACs will say, 'We want people to walk in our shoes'" (Coleman 2016b). Exhibit text reflects the commitment to community perspective. Wing Luke Museum staff consider themselves community facilitators, preferring to listen to community voices instead of amplifying their views. Exhibits at the Wing Luke Museum are developed through the CBEM, a process that begins with an "Initial Outreach" stage in which museum staff members reach out to a potential partner, a local Asian Pacific American community, to build rapport (Coleman 2016b). As relationships build between the Wing Luke Museum and the potential community partner, the museum staff listen to the "current issues and events community members are passionate about" (Chinn 2006a, 15). The Wing Luke Museum holds steadfast to the words of John Cotton Dana and has learned what its community needs and has fit its mission to meet those needs. During the outreach section, a recruitment process is held to create a Community Advisory Committee (CAC) that will develop and prioritize the themes and messages for the exhibit. The CAC will also act as an advocate for the museum to collect objects and oral histories from the community (Chinn 2006a, 15). The museum staff of the Wing Luke and the CAC work together to find the "authentic voice—a first-person voice" for the exhibits. Oral history techniques are a key component of selection, with CAC members occasionally completing "oral history training so they're interviewing their family members." In recruiting community partners for object and oral history collection, the Wing Luke Museum has avoided *the hindrance of the physicality of the museum.* The objects and stories of the Wing Luke Museum are not isolated; they are interwoven into the life of the nearby communities. The community has handled the items on display and heard the stories of the exhibition, and they are a physical part of the museum. The nearby community is not simply a donor to the museum; the CAC shapes and serves as a resource for content. The museum staff is responsible for designing the display and highlighting the selected objects and stories according to the community's wishes.

At the Wing Luke Museum, *community health and well-being come first,* a sentiment echoed by its curators:

> For us here at the museum, again we're working hand in hand with communities, we respect that there's a certain time and readiness within a community to tell their story. And sometimes that rubs roughly with an individual scholar—who is like, "we need to tell the truth—we need to tell the full picture of what happened." Our choice instead is to allow communities time and readiness because it brings in that element . . . of healing and it's not my role to decide which stories a community should or should not tell about themselves. I can provide a platform for that but it's the community and the individual's decision on that. So I need to be honoring of that. (Coleman 2016b)

The Community-Based Exhibition Model ensures that participant communities are empowered and reflects the core values of the Wing Luke Museum, including "We (the museum staff) willingly relinquish control" (Coleman 2016b). Shared curatorial authority and the emphasis on community empowerment is visible throughout the museum, providing a platform for discussion of social and political issues and encouraging social justice advocacy. The Wing Luke Museum is capable of handling difficult issues because it shares authority with community partners.

The Wing Luke Museum is a "national model for community-based exhibition development and oral history gathering projects" (Chinn 2016). In 1995, the Wing Luke Museum was recognized by the Institute for Museum and Library Services (IMLS), receiving the National Award for Museum Service for "fostering broad-based participation in the development of exhibitions and programs." The Community-Based Exhibition Model is time intensive, with an exhibition development process that "involves many community members over the course of 12–18 months" (Chinn 2016). The Wing Luke Museum has adopted the transformation process of *time is at the disposal of all*, and this patience has led to a viable community museum. One museum staff member spoke of the *intentionally democratic* "process behind—there's all these voices coming forward—they (museum visitors) do feel like they come here, they meet real people, they experience something authentic—whatever that means. And I believe that comes directly from our process of making" (Coleman 2016b). As an inclusive institution, the Wing Luke Museum has overcome the obstacles that block most museums from strong community partnerships and, in doing so, has remained relevant to its community for fifty years.

Proposed Evaluation Techniques
for Tier 2 Inclusive Museums

The traditional quantitative techniques such as visitor surveying and exhibition studies work well for analyzing the inclusivity of a tier 1 inclusive museum. Yet, in a tier 2 museum, what should you be looking for? When I examine a tier 2 inclusive museum, I examine instances in which shared curatorial voice is the *direct intention* of the museum; multiple voices can be heard within curatorial voice; democracy is practiced; museum professionals address on multiple levels social exclusion; and museums have formed community partnerships. I collect quantitative data such as demographics, attendance numbers, and collection metadata. I compare the quantitative findings with longitudinal studies of the general population, looking for the museum's impact upon community health and well-being. I also rely on qualitative techniques such as interviewing and ethnographic studies. I examine qualitatively the perceptions of museum visitors and staff concerning exhibits, collections, community issues, and the role of

Figure 5.4.   Proposed Evaluation Techniques of Tier 2 Inclusion.
Created by Laura-Edythe Coleman.

the museum. I outline my favorite quantitative and qualitative techniques in chapter 8.

Inclusion through Community Partnerships

As American museums grow into their role as inclusive institutions, they will expand their work beyond the first tier—partnerships with people—to the second tier and form bonds with community programs. This second leve of inclusive museum practice faces several hindrances, such as clashes over institutional identity and curatorial authority. Ultimately, museum professionals can employ transformational processes such as the Community-Based Exhibition Model to create and solidify community connections. These community partnerships will form the structure of the third-tier museum, the vehicle for broad social change. In the next chapter we will explore the ways in which museums become that vehicle and create change with their communities.

6

Driving Broad Social Change

Becoming a Vehicle

Museums performing on the first tier of social inclusion successfully partner with individuals to provide cultural inclusion. The impact of the first tier is specific: target individuals who will then carry your message out into the community. A step beyond the individual level is tier 2: partnerships with programs. At the second tier, your museum can not only impact individuals but also pair with social organizations to benefit community health. While these two levels are excellent goals for American museums to reach, there is yet another level to strive for: the vehicle of broad social change. This third level is rarely attained by any institution and is particularly difficult for museums. What is this vehicle of broad social change? How do our museums become that vehicle? Why is it so difficult to evolve into this type of museum? In this chapter, I will explore the highly contested notion of the museum as a propulsion agent for social change. I will present examples of museums that, acting as change agents, have debunked the myth of museum neutrality. I will also examine the two main types of museums in this third tier: first, those born with a social agenda; second, those that adopt a social agenda. As you read this chapter, I challenge you to consider the type of change that your museum could advance within society.

What on Earth Is a
"Vehicle for Broad Social Change"?

In 1998, Richard Sandell described this third tier of the socially inclusive museum as "the vehicle for broad social change" (Sandell 1998, 401–18). This type of museum aimed to "influence society/instigate positive social change" (Sandell 1998, 401–18). A museum at this level goes beyond achieving a single community outcome such as "heart health awareness" and increasing local participation in CPR courses. A museum driving social change will take a stand on contentious social issues such as immigration, race, inequity, and injustice. Museums tackle social issues as tier 2 institutions by forming partnerships with community programs and as tier 1 institutions by partnering with people. A tier 3 inclusive museum will build on those partnerships and take a stand on broader issues. For instance, a level three museum might take a stand on gender equality in America, and as part of this stance, the museum would partner with community organizations with similar goals: National Committee on Pay Equity, National Organization for Women, local trade unions, the American Civil Liberties Union, and local rape crisis centers. A museum at level three will also partner with individuals on the social issue: exhibits on pay gaps and dissemination of legal information to combat discrimination. The UK DCMS labels this third level "third stage: museums, galleries, and archives as agents of social change" (DCMS 2000, 1–36). I argue that a museum operating in the third tier will, by necessity, be undertaking tiers 1 and 2. In my model, your museum does not leave its two inclusions to become tier 3. Instead, higher levels build upon lower ones and incorporate their activities within level three. Additionally, your museum may be at different levels on multiple issues. For example, your museum may be exceptionally adept at level one partnerships with people, but only on specific themes related to the community for level two. In a level three museum, you will be attempting to create social change across all of your exhibits, programming, and collections. Please note that in all of these levels, it will take tremendous effort to attain inclusion, but it is possible if you scaffold your approach.

How Does the Third-Tier Museum Function as an Agent of Broad Social Change?

Sandell suggests that the "museum as the vehicle for broad social change" will achieve this goal by "providing a forum for public debate, education, and persuasion" (Sandell 1998, 401–18). This museum type publicly acknowledges its societal role unashamedly. You can imagine at this point that level three museums are hard to find: "Those museums which clearly articulate their purpose in relation to society and which purposefully seek to position themselves as organizations with a part to play in multi-agency solutions for tackling social exclusion are nevertheless still rare" (Sandell 1998, 401–18). A tier 3 inclusive museum will tackle exclusion in all four dimensions simultaneously: cultural, economic, social, and political. Specifically, a tier 3 museum will be both a level one and a level two museum; be aligned with greater social frameworks when possible; have an articulated inclusive purpose in their mission/vision/philosophy statements published; and be able to demonstrate benefits and outcomes of their inclusive impact upon society (see figure 6.1).

After accomplishing the first and second levels, the third-tier museum is poised to connect with greater social frameworks. Seek out the city, state, local, and national government guidelines for inclusiveness. Study the specific goals your governments may have related to inclusion. Make sure that your museum meets, if not exceeds, the goals outlined by government policy. To be fair, the United States does not have inclusion goals articulated consistently in government policy. The United Kingdom has developed social inclusion policies and guidelines to assist cultural institutions such as museums. In the area that your museum resides, there may be few government policies to connect the work of your museum to. In the absence of such policies, I propose that you look to the guidelines of UK policy. In doing so, you will have a recognizable point in public policy to refer to your inclusion work. In other words, if you do not have government policies dictating how inclusive your institutions should be, you must look to alternative verifiable sources, such as the UK guidelines. It may become necessary in the future

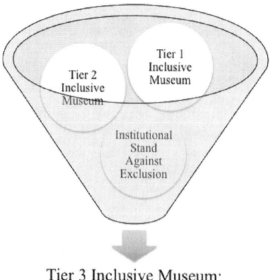

Tier 3 Inclusive Museum:
Driving Broad Social Change

Figure 6.1.   Attributes of a Tier 3 Inclusive Museum.
Created by Laura-Edythe Coleman.

to know "where your museum stands in a large service framework" to obtain funding (DCMS 2000, 1–36). Currently, the UK policies for inclusion are the gold standard. To research UK policies on inclusion, please see the resources at the end of the book.

A key attribute of the third-tier inclusive museum is that you will have articulated with your museum's main mission or vision statement a commitment to inclusion. Your museum can be an agent of social change but will be more successfully so when your museum publicly states what its social role is. For example, the Tyne and Wear Museum vision statement reads, "The vision for the future of TWM is for: Total Inclusion" (DCMS 2000, 1–36). This museum, like others, states publicly and clearly that inclusion is a priority—in this case, TWM has inclusion at the top of its list of goals. Are these lofty, unattainable goals? I do not believe so. Does the Tyne and Wear Museum leave any doubt as to its purpose? No, TWM clearly articulates its social role. Is this a broad statement? Yes, I have to admit that a vision statement such as the TWM vision statement is subjective, but it is a good starting place, and my experience has been that those museums that clearly state their goals, no matter how lofty, have a greater chance of reaching their achievements.

According to the UK publication *Holding Up the Mirror*, the "mission statement of the museum should address the commitment and the responsibility of reflecting cultural heritages and shared futures of the community" (Denniston, Langham, and Martin 2003). Notice that this publication is not stressing the traditional purposes of the museum—collections—but social responsibility. What would your museum's mission statement look like if it contained the social purpose of inclusion? For example, the Portland Art Museum "strives to be an inclusive institution that facilitates respectful dialogue, debate and the free exchange of ideas" (Portland Art Museum). Take a few moments to review

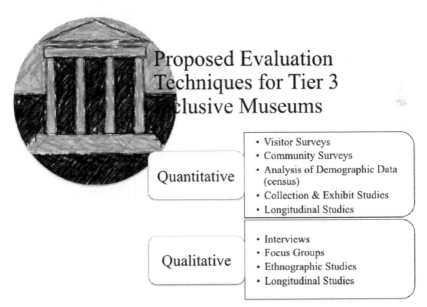

Figure 6.2.   *Proposed Evaluation Techniques of Tier 3 Inclusion.*
Created by Laura-Edythe Coleman.

the tools for inclusion in chapter 4, and consider possible rewordings of your institution's mission and vision statements.

Successful tier 3 museums have thoughtfully developed measurements for the social impact of their museums. I understand that measuring success seems far off in the future, but, I assure you, your museum must decide in advance how to measure the inclusive impact of your institution upon society. I am not alone in suggesting that measurements of success be determined at the onset, or before, the implementation of inclusive practices (Scott 2013). UK government agencies state, "It is therefore crucial that objectives and criteria for success and performance indicators are set at the onset and regularly reviewed and evaluated" (DCMS 2000, 1–36). I propose in my adaptation of Sandell's typology that this third-level inclusive museum performs longitudinal studies to monitor museum impact upon the community (see figure 6.2).

Born versus Transformed

It has been nearly twenty years since Sandell stated that this third-level inclusive museum is "nevertheless still rare" (Sandell 1998a, 401–18). Unfortunately, this is still the case. While the number of museums impacting their communities through inclusive practices has increased, most museums have centered their efforts around tiers 1 and 2. Quite simply, a museum acting so completely as an agent of social change is unusual. There are two main types of level three inclusive museums: those institutions "born" inclusive and those institutions "transformed into" inclusive museums. As mentioned previously, most American museums will fall into the latter category. It bears mentioning that those institutions "born" or created to be inclusive are, from day one, acting as vehicles that drive broad social change.

"Born" Inclusive

Is it the wave of the future to create museums that are based predominately on "experiences" rather than collections (Weil

1999, 2002)? Many museum theorists have postulated that recently created museums tend to lean more toward experiential, informal learning environments. The question I hear the most is one based in disbelief: "How do you build a museum without a collection?" Do we have the ability to make a museum without a collection of objects or art? The museum professionals of the National Center for Civil and Human Rights would probably say that we could create such an institution. And what's more, the institution would probably be a success.

Example: The National Center for Civil and Human Rights

The National Center for Civil and Human Rights (NCCHR) is located in downtown Atlanta, Georgia. The museum opened to the public in 2014 and features permanent and temporary exhibits but has no formal collections.

Tier 1 Inclusion

The NCCHR is first-tier inclusive: individuals are activated to be agents of social change. Each curator described themselves as facilitators and translators—personnel that assists museum visitors in the crafting of curatorial voice. There are multiple "layers of voices" expressed throughout the Center, demonstrating a merging of individual stories into collective identity in *Collective Stories* (Coleman 2016b). One curator spoke of this merging: "As we layer more and more in, again I think that strengthens our curatorial voice" (Coleman 2016b). Both curators interviewed believed that the Center represented voices that could not "survive the mainstream voice" (Coleman 2016b). The curator participants stressed the importance of bringing in the voices of those traditionally marginalized. "We have to bring the voices of undocumented students, we have to bring the voices of human trafficking survivors, we have to bring in *all of these voices*" (Coleman 2016b). The inclusion of multiple voices, especially of those traditionally marginalized, allows for the NCCHR to provide a *personal* experience, a key element of a tier 1 inclusive museum.

In particular, these curators worked together to create a pamphlet, "Across Generations: Intergenerational Conversation Starters." This pamphlet is designed to "inspire intergenerational dialogue that lasts long after you visit The Center" (National Center for Civil and Human Rights 2015). Parents and caregivers are encouraged to discuss the nature of civil rights, human rights, power, and control. The pamphlet emphasizes the importance of "connecting the past and the present" (National Center for Civil and Human Rights 2015). As with many of the experiences of the NCCHR, this pamphlet is intended to promote inclusion that is *portable*—a key component of a tier 1 inclusive museum.

The NCCHR provides experiences that are *personal* and *participatory* by explaining the struggle for civil and human rights through an immersive museum visitor experience. As warned in the signage, some of the material presented is of a graphic nature and not appropriate for younger visitors. At these graphic exhibits, museum personnel await to assist visitors and to chaperone those experiencing the more emotional content. The exhibition *Rolls Down Like Water: The American Civil Rights Movement*

Figure 6.3.   NCCHR Lunch Counter Image.

contains an immersive "lunch counter" experience. Museum visitors sit at the lunch counter, reenacting the role of a "sit-in" protestor during segregation. The museum visitor wears a set of headphones and places their hands upon the lunch counter, and instantly a timer begins on a digital clock. As the seconds tick by, the museum visitor listens to the verbal abuse of the lunch counter piped into their ears. The combination of verbal abuse and the shaking chair (simulating a physical thrashing from the angry crowd) is intense, and museum visitors appear visibly shaken by the experience. During the "soft opening" of the museum, the curators discovered the absolute necessity of maintaining a "chaperone" at the lunch counter—a museum docent ready to calm upset museum visitors and offer facial tissues. The NCCHR provides *participatory* experiences for museum visitors, a cornerstone of tier 1 inclusion.

Tier 2 Inclusion

The NCCHR is second-tier inclusive, teaming up with other like-minded social organizations, such as CARE, to fight global poverty. The NCCHR curators emphasize the importance of *localization* by "using Atlanta as a focal point" (Coleman 2016b). The Center features the "narratives that are being told with the Atlanta community," and one curator noted, "We highlight civil rights in Atlanta . . . it's something that they're going to need to relate to on a local level as they look at the national level picture" (Coleman 2016b). The curators spoke of localization as a mechanism for bringing people out from their "bubble" or their "own backyard" to see things on a larger, but always personal, scale (Coleman 2016b).

Tier 3 Inclusion

The NCCHR is third-tier inclusive, clearly articulating a social purpose for its museum, one that is inclusive of "all" people. The mission of the Center is "to empower people to take the protection of every human's rights personally. Through sharing stories of courage and struggle around the world, The Center

Figure 6.4.   NCCHR Partnerships.

encourages visitors to gain a deeper understanding of the role they play in helping to protect the rights of all people" (National Center for Civil and Human Rights 2014).

How Does the NCCHR Accomplish Its Social Goals?

The second floor and entrance to the museum contains the permanent exhibit *Rolls Down Like Water: The American Civil Rights Movement*. This exhibit is described as an "experience," and museum visitors are invited to "experience the brave fight for equality in the modern American Civil Rights Movement as told by Tony Award–winning exhibition curator George C. Wolfe" (National Center for Civil and Human Rights 2014). One NCCHR curator indicated that the theatrical background of Mr. Wolfe allowed for closer attention to "the dynamics of light and darkness and sound and silence" than one might find in a more traditional museum setting (National Center for Civil and Human Rights 2014). Unlike the traditional museum, the NCCHR does not own a large collection of civil rights–related artifacts. Instead, the story of the

American civil rights movement is co-constructed with museum visitors through a series of intense experiences.

The third floor contains the permanent but routinely updated exhibit *Spark of Conviction: The Global Human Rights Movement*, in which museum visitors "come face to face with human rights champions" (National Center for Civil and Human Rights 2014). The Center explores current human rights issues such as child labor, human trafficking, and the exploitation of undocumented workers. The presentation of local and global problems is accompanied by a push for museum visitors to take action—to become social justice advocates. In this exhibit, the museum visitor is invited to leave a video testimony for the museum's "Collective Stories Wall."

The only level of the NCCHR that contains artifacts is the first floor and basement level of the Center, which houses temporary exhibits such as the *Voice to the Voiceless: The Morehouse College Martin Luther King, Jr., Collection*. This area of the museum is traditional in appearance with glass cases, lighting, and object labels. If you are expecting a standard museum visit, this level is a good entry point for traditional museum visitors. It is important to note that this traditional museum exhibit area is small, and it is placed within the context of the museum as an agent of social change.

Shared Curatorial Authority

In the NCCHR, curators share authority with the museum visitor in unique ways.

The NCCHR curators are open to relinquishing control over the curatorial voice of the exhibits, stating, "I think that curatorial voice has many dialects asare in the world . . . there's definitely a spectrum . . . in terms of people giving up control of curatorial voice—the other side of that—letting in the community, letting in other experts to be part of making that voice" (Coleman 2016b). For the curators, the timbres and tones of curatorial voice are produced in a collective effort—fulfilling the mission of the Center. Not only do the curators of the NCCHR share curatorial voice, but they also listen intently for the new curatorial voice being developed by museum visitors.

Listening for the Co-creation of Curatorial Voice

NCCHR curators state that they listened for "what individual people around me are saying," or "I think I naturally am listening with my ears but also with my eyes . . . when I go to other exhibitions, I hear what other people are saying" (Coleman 2016b). NCCHR curators reported actively *eavesdropping* as a format for the discerning of *curatorial voice* within an exhibit. In particular, one noted, "This idea of across generations—I think it's a success and I become very intrigued with adults who are talking to children, children who are talking to adults . . . that's success for the museum, that people are talking about their experiences and making connections" (Coleman 2016b). This curator interviewee further indicated that her listening watched for "whenever you find people having a conversation around something—it could be an object, it could be a painting, it could be a panel—that is usually a sign." Her active listening sought out, visually, for "someone standing for more than 30 seconds," because, as she explained, that visitor pause indicated "that is an important space for them" (Coleman 2016b). The curators of NCCHR indicated that they would like to find ways to move the museum further along the "spectrum of radical trust, really allowing community people to be heard" (Coleman 2016b). Instead of a planned "progression" of the exhibits, the NCCHR allows visitors to find their own way without the use of *directionality of exhibits*: "We don't have a set path, and we don't have a storyline that has to be told in the exact same way, that it is really about people finding their own story in their own path" (Coleman 2016b).

Choosing to Take an Institutional Stand

From the inception of NCCHR, guiding principles concerning the social role of the museum have been in place. These principles, which extend beyond the mission and vision statements of the organization, shape the exhibitions. This curator interviewee spoke of the principles thusly:

> Basic principles which include: historians we love you but we're not creating this for you—so there's not going to be a

history book within the exhibitions. People who lived through the Civil Rights Movement, this exhibition space isn't for you either—they've always said it's really for the people who did not live through the experience, so based on design and voice. (Coleman 2016b)

The curators of the NCCHR openly admit that this institution is nontraditional and born inclusive, acknowledging that "it is not a traditional 'we collect, we preserve, we disseminate'" (Coleman 2016b). This is particularly evident when museum visitors contrast their experiences in the temporary Martin Luther King Jr. gallery with the greater museum:

The only place you see actual documents and authentic objects is in the Martin Luther King gallery. And so for us, the objects take a back seat to the story and the conversations that start which is something again that various museums are experimenting and playing with but definitely not a traditional trajectory. (Coleman 2016b)

The curators further reflected upon the nontraditional nature of the Center, noting that they attempt to blend or integrate their mission into the fabric of society, empowering individuals to "take the protection of everyone's human rights personally." One curator directly linked *integration* to the social advocacy role of the museum, stating that "integration is probably something we talk about a lot with our social justice mission; really, we are using our exhibitions as a discussion point, conversation starters, not in and of themselves."

Traditional Museums "Transformed" into Inclusive Museums

As the majority of American museums are already established as traditional institutions of collections and exhibitions, we must seek dynamic ways of transforming our museums into inclusive institutions. This type of transformation does not happen overnight. The process to become the third-tier inclusive institutions will take years, not months. Museums that have held to traditional models of functioning will struggle to make change occur. Real change takes time in any institution, and museums are no different. How can we achieve third-tier inclusion when we are a traditional museum?

Example: The New-York Historical Society Museum & Library

The NYHS, founded in 1804, is the oldest museum in New York City. It is by all accounts a traditional institution containing collections, conserving items, and promoting access to information. It is not bound to these traditional activities. Over the years, the NYHS has stretched its work to range across a number of socially purposeful activities. In doing so, the NYHS has become both a tier 1 and a tier 2 inclusive museum. How does a historical society remain relevant to current events? And how does such an organization act in an inclusive manner? The NYHS has developed inventive ways to reach new audiences while adhering to its mission statement: "To serve as a national forum for the discussion of issues surrounding the making and meaning of history" (New-York Historical Society "About").

Example: The Citizenship Project

An excellent example of the NYHS's ability to evolve its message is the Citizenship Project, "a major initiative to help the more than one million legal immigrants in the New York region become American citizens through free civics and American history classes and other educational and digital learning tools" (New-York Historical Society "The Citizenship Project"). This project is no small undertaking and builds upon many of the NYHS's previously existing education programs, exhibits, and resources such as books and films. This evolution took time, a decade of the NYHS museum serving as host for naturalization ceremonies, and "the idea for the program had been germinating since 2004 when the historical society began hosting naturalization ceremonies, and the process was jump-started in January when President Trump issued his first travel ban" (Fuhrmans and Blumenthal 2017). One process built upon another, and now the NYHS offers free classes to immigrants preparing for their American history and civics exams.

Tier 1 Inclusion

The NYHS changes individual lives through the Citizenship Project. It is the ultimate act of inclusion to assist immigrants in their quest for citizenship. The Citizenship Project is *personal, participatory,* and *portable.* The NYHS meets personal needs by offering classes at a variety of times such as evening, weekday, and weekend immersion programs (Voon). The Citizenship Project is participatory through use of the NYHS physical collection and programming, such as scavenger hunts throughout the museum exhibits (Levy). In fact, the "program is so unique that citizenship and immigration services has invited the museum to host a seminar showing other museums across the country how to establish similar programs" (Fuhrmans and Blumenthal 2017). The Citizenship Project is extremely portable: the museum visitors that participate take the museum's message with them into their communities, and what's more, they come back to the museum (Levy).

Tier 2 Inclusion

The NYHS did not embark upon the Citizenship Project alone: the museum formed partnerships with key social organizations. In particular, the NYHS partnered with the City University of New York's Citizenship Now! program, which "offers free and confidential immigration law services" (Voon; Levy; CUNY). Additionally, the NYHS received funding from the Ford Foundation, the Andrew W. Mellon Foundation, and the New York Community Trust (Voon; Levy; CUNY). A major social change project such as the Citizenship Project could not have been undertaken by the NYHS alone, and the partnerships with like-minded social organizations demonstrated wisdom on the part of the museum.

Tier 3 Inclusion

The third tier of inclusion requires that an institution articulate its social change agenda. NYHS CEO and president Dr. Louise Mirrer says it best: "At New-York Historical, we believe in an inclusive 'We the People,' welcoming immigrants as well as those born in the United States to a nation whose motto is, after all, *E Pluribus Unum*—out of many, one" (Levy). The NYHS is taking a stand and, with that stand, political risks. The current political climate within the United States does not favor immigration and naturalization. The NYHS embraces immigration and continues to provide a pathway for citizenship through inclusive programming. This is the hallmark of a traditional museum transformed into an inclusive museum.

A Word about the Diversity and Inclusion Policies

I recommend against adding a diversity and inclusion policy to your museum's documents unless you are immediately ready to begin work in such areas. For many institutions, the traditional D&I policy is nothing more than a sticker slapped on to museum paperwork. When a D&I policy is added, society will always see inclusion work as secondary to the main goals of your museum. And as long your inclusion policy is secondary to your work, your museum will remain exclusive.

The Journey to Tier 3 Inclusive Museums

American museums are capable of becoming third-level inclusive institutions, either by transformation or by birth into inclusive practices. We must acknowledge that these changes will not happen quickly, that we must be willing to work steadily, and that for every milestone we would like to see our museum meet, we should plan on having several stepping-stones instead of giant leaps to get there.

7

Tools for Implementing Inclusion in Your Museum

American museums are not prepared to implement inclusion. We simply have not developed the tools needed by museum professionals to accomplish this task. We are not teaching our graduate students in museum studies programs how to make their museums more inclusive. We have the occasional AAM webinar, and our national conference has been buzzing with programs titled with the term *inclusion*. Yet I would argue that only a very few American museum professionals, researchers, and theorists are actually developing tools to implement inclusion. What type of tools do we need? Who should teach us about inclusion for museums? Where can we go for help? In this chapter, I offer practical advice to start you on your journey. Be advised, I truly believe that there is much more work to be done in the development of inclusive tools.

What Type of Tools Do We Need?

If we are to create inclusive institutions, we must develop tools that meet the needs of each of the tiers outlined in chapters 4, 5, and 6. As you can imagine, the tools necessary for each of these levels will vary. To accomplish level one inclusion, the tools are designed to enhance our relationships with individuals—specifically, the relationship between your museum and your visitor. Second-level inclusion requires tools that expand the relationships of your museum beyond individual members of the public to partner with pre-existing community programs. To achieve third-level inclusion, we will need to develop tools together to change the ways in which American museums impact society.

Tools for Level One Inclusion

What tools can help our museums to attain level one inclusion? Fortunately for us, several tools already exist. The tools that I will outline are exemplars of the kind of professional guidelines that our field is capable of producing. The list provided here is not exhaustive, but it is intended to motivate you, the museum professional, to consider the types of tools you would like to create in the future.

Margaret Middleton's Family-Inclusive Language Chart

In 2014, Margaret Middleton created a poster chart that details the best practices for family-inclusive language (Middleton "Including the 21st Century Family"). This chart is downloadable as a .pdf and also available for order from her website. The significance of her work is not simply that you now have a tool for assisting in family inclusiveness; it is that you will be prompted to think critically about the ways in which you identify your museum visitors. Her chart outlines words and phrases you should avoid in speaking with museum visitors; an explanation of why you should not use such words; and what are acceptable language substitutes (see figure 7.1). Middleton's work will push you and your museum to see individual museum visitors on a *personal* level. By implementing her suggestions when engaging the public, you will be better able to elicit participation from your museum visitors. Ultimately, you want your museum visitors to walk away from your museum carrying your message as their own. You cannot accomplish this ultimate goal of *portability*

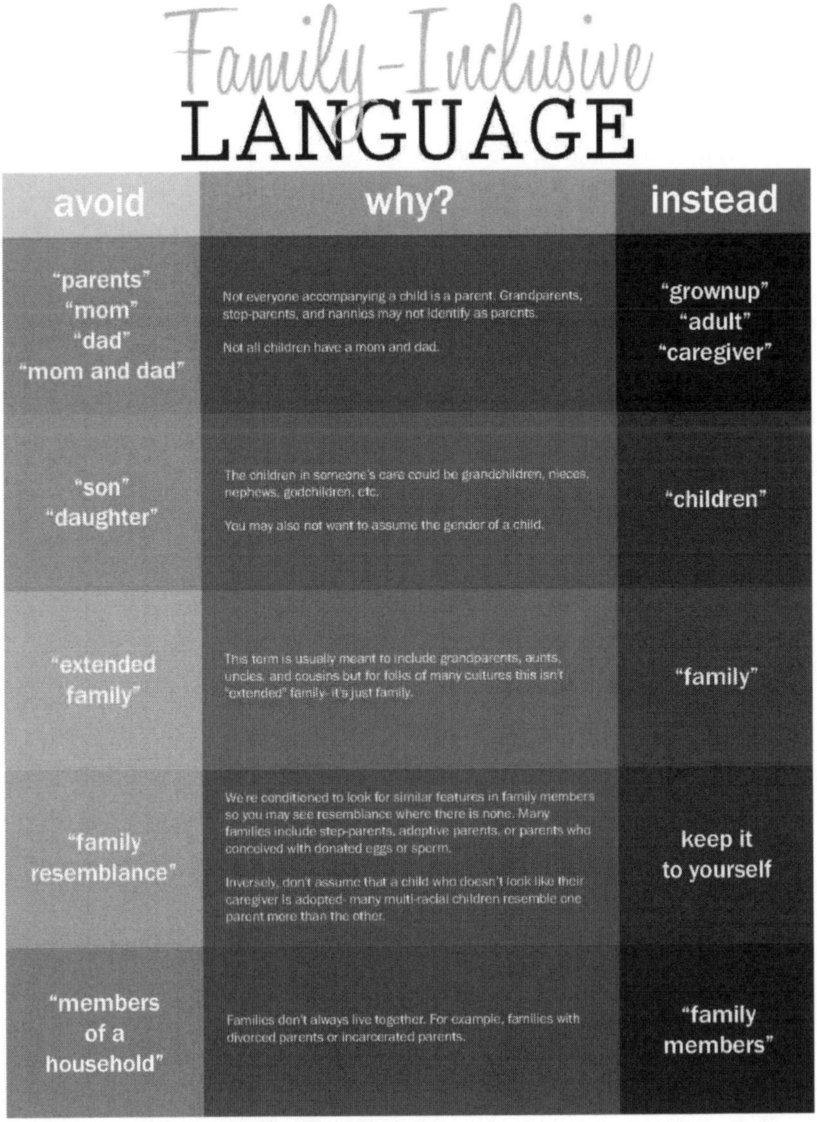

Family-Inclusive
LANGUAGE

avoid	why?	instead
"parents" "mom" "dad" "mom and dad"	Not everyone accompanying a child is a parent. Grandparents, step-parents, and nannies may not identify as parents. Not all children have a mom and dad.	"grownup" "adult" "caregiver"
"son" "daughter"	The children in someone's care could be grandchildren, nieces, nephews, godchildren, etc. You may also not want to assume the gender of a child.	"children"
"extended family"	This term is usually meant to include grandparents, aunts, uncles, and cousins but for folks of many cultures this isn't "extended" family- it's just family.	"family"
"family resemblance"	We're conditioned to look for similar features in family members so you may see resemblance where there is none. Many families include step-parents, adoptive parents, or parents who conceived with donated eggs or sperm. Inversely, don't assume that a child who doesn't look like their caregiver is adopted- many multi-racial children resemble one parent more than the other.	keep it to yourself
"members of a household"	Families don't always live together. For example, families with divorced parents or incarcerated parents.	"family members"

Figure 7.1. Margaret Middleton's Chart.
Middleton, "Including the 21st Century Family."

if you do not recognize your museum visitors for who they are. Take a few minutes to ponder Middleton's chart, and consider the places in your museum's language where you could make appropriate changes. Then dialogue with your colleagues about other language that you may use in your museum—you may find other terms that need to be more inclusive!

Taboo Incluseum Edition

Few websites rival Incluseum.com for depth and breadth of inclusive resources. In addition, the Incluseum's resources are entirely free to download and use. The Taboo Incluseum Edition is a simple card game to increase awareness of inclusion among museum staff. Again, this is a resource focused on language. In particular, this game is intended to help your museum understand that the words we use to describe the social work of a museum (inclusion, diversity, community, accessibility) are subjective and, as such, mean different things to different people. I recommend that you use this tool as a starting point and add other subjective terms. Encourage your colleagues to debate the meaning of these terms.

LGTBQ Alliance Welcoming Guidelines for Museums

This 2016 publication contains "concrete tools to help museums incorporate LGBTQ diversity and inclusion into their understanding and pursuit of excellence." This document offers a checklist for your museum that includes both the Standard Recommendation from AAM and the LGBTQ Welcoming Guidelines. As you and your museum work through this checklist, you will see the ways in which your museum can improve. These tools are just the beginning of how museum professionals could change their mindsets and, in doing so, alter the inclusivity of their museum. Why do these tools work to make museums first-level inclusive? These tools are designed to hone your focus in on the needs of individual museum visitors. Once you center your museum work on individuals, you will be on your way to inclusion level one.

Tools for Tier 2 Inclusion

Are there blueprints for museum–community organization partnerships? Yes, there are plenty of blueprints, tools, and resources available online. There is an abundance of case studies and example programs throughout the United States. As a museum professional, you may find conference presentations and interactions with other museum professionals who have experience in museum–community partnerships to be helpful. Despite the unique nature of every museum, and each community, there are clear ways to produce strong museum–community program bonds.

Museum/Community Partnerships: Lessons Learned from the Bridges Conference

From understanding "Pitfalls & Possibilities" to "Strategies for Attaining Financial Sustainability," this free publication outlines the process of building a museum–community program partnership. The document blends practitioner insights with strong theoretical literature, providing a clear pathway for your museum to connect with community programs. See the resources section of this book.

NISE Museum and Community Partnerships: Collaboration Guide

The National Informal Stem Education Network developed a collaboration guide for "museums working with community youth-serving organizations" (McCarthy and Herring 2015). This guidebook is available for free download, along with several sample forms and templates that will benefit your museum. In this document, you will master the process of building museum–community program partnerships. In addition, this guidebook contains "Profiles of National Youth-Serving Organizations," an essential "who's who" in nonprofit organizations for youth (McCarthy and Herring 2015). Of particular use are the "collaboration tips" and how to write a "memorandum of understanding" between your museum and your community partners (McCarthy and Herring 2015). For more information, please see the resources section of this book.

Tools for Tier 3 Inclusion

Level three inclusion is extremely difficult to attain; yet it has been done. The Wing Luke Museum has generated all of its exhibits using the Community-Based Exhibition Model (CBEM). This model was developed by Wing Luke Museum curator Cassie Chinn and has remained in use for several decades. The CBEM has proven successful time and time again, resulting in the adoption of this model by other institutions such as the Arab American National Museum and the Japanese American National Museum. Why does this model work? And who exactly is the "community" in the Community-Based Exhibition Model?

The CBEM works for museums because it involves community members at every stage of the process. Instead of creating exhibits for communities, museums like the Wing Luke Museum co-create exhibits with their communities. Unlike the traditional museum, the Wing Luke Museum has engaged in the CBEM, a format that "builds upon a basic exhibition development model but strives to infuse community members throughout the entire process" (Chinn 2006a). A glance at the Wing Luke Museum website's "Exhibit Team" reveals the significance of community members in the exhibition process; "each Exhibit Team generally includes: Museum staff; Core community members; Participating community members" (Chinn 2016). Does your museum's exhibition team contain community members? Do nonmuseum personnel account for two-thirds of your exhibit team? Why or why not?

Often I am asked, "But who are the community?" This is a reasonable question to ask, and one that we should never stop asking as museum professionals. In the example of the Wing Luke Museum, the museum staff has intentionally left the "definition of community pretty open" (Coleman 2016b).

Quite frankly, I suggest that your museum consider leaving the definition of community open as well. Allow your community to define themselves. I firmly believe that such openness will lead to a better relationship with your community. For example, the Wing Luke Museum has had tremendous success in defining "community" as "people who live in the Seattle area" (Chinn 2016). What roles do community members take on in the CBEM? Primarily, exhibits designed using the CBEM require the creation of a Community Advisory Committee (CAC); typically ten to fifteen individuals serve as the primary decision makers and are charged with developing the main messages, themes, content, and form of the exhibit and its related components. The CAC also connects the project to other community members by inviting others to join the CAC; sharing about the project with family members, peers, and community contacts; suggesting individuals for oral histories and artifacts, photographs, and document loans; and helping gather materials. Oftentimes, individuals on the CAC or others they know will write the exhibit text, create an exhibit video, take new photographs to showcase oral history participants and/or community life, serve on an artwork selection panel, provide graphic design services, and more (Chinn 2006a).

Is your museum willing to relinquish control to your community? For more information, please see the resources section and the appendix located at the back of this book.

Inclusiveness at Work: How to Build Inclusive Nonprofit Organizations

This document, freely available for download, is a detailed handbook for training your organization to become more inclusive. Included in this book are worksheets, assessments, training materials, frameworks, and a blueprint for creating an inclusive nonprofit organization (Denver Foundation). While not specifically written for museums, the materials within this book are an excellent resource for any museum seeking to become an inclusive organization. See the resources section for further information.

Who Should Teach Us about Inclusion for Museums?

How can we learn more about inclusion? Who is qualified to provide a thorough understanding of inclusion to our museums? First and foremost, I suggest that graduate training programs are an excellent place to begin the formation of informed museum practice. I propose that the American museum profession examine closely the University of Leicester's new program in Socially Engaged Practice in Museums and Galleries (University of Leicester). Despite the fact that Leicester's program of study is UK based, it also "draws on broader global shifts in practice" and, as such, has applications outside of the United Kingdom (University of Leicester). American graduate museum studies programs should develop courses to better explain the social role of the museum and expand the abilities of their graduates with the skills to become agents of social change. New graduate museum studies programs in inclusion for museums could be created, and existing programs such as those at Johns Hopkins University and George Washington University could be enhanced by inclusivity training.

What If We Cannot Go Back to School?

The majority of museum professionals are busy completing their daily tasks and do not have the time or finances to attend graduate school, often for the second time. Professional organizations such as the American Alliance of Museums must help bridge the gap for current museum practitioners by providing training in inclusivity. How can AAM provide training? The American Alliance of Museums has begun to offer webinars on inclusion, but this is not enough. I propose that AAM provide training that can equate to continuing education credits for current museum professionals. Such training should be accounted for in museum efforts to maintain AAM accreditation. Overall, I believe that AAM must take a stand with the field and proclaim the importance of inclusion for museums.

Who Can Help My Museum?

There are increasing numbers of qualified consultants available for hire. The abilities of these consultants vary by experience and education, but one common thread links all of these individuals: an unwavering commitment to the inclusive role of the museum. (For a complete list of consultants available at the time of publication, please see the resources section.) Museums and museum professionals have several viable options for further information that does not involve training. In particular, the Inclusive Museum Knowledge Community and Incluseum.com are excellent resources for your museum. The Inclusive Museum Knowledge Community is available online, at onmuseums.com, for "exploring the future role of museums, with a particular focus on how they can become more inclusive" (Inclusive Museum). This Knowledge Community is also responsible for an in-print publication, *The International Journal of the Inclusive Museum*. This publication is a fantastic source of theoretical, historical, and practical information concerning inclusion for museums. Additionally, this Knowledge Community hosts an annual international conference, a several-day event that illuminates the social role of the museum and provides museum practitioners with networking opportunities. I am a regular attendee of the Inclusive Museum Conference, and I recommend this exceptional gathering to anyone interested in inclusive practices for museums. The next conference will be in 2018 and will have the theme "Special Focus—Inclusion as Shared Vision: Museums and Sharing Heritage."

Another online venue for inclusive resources is the Incluseum .com. Founded in 2012 by Aletheia Wittman and Rose Paquet Kinsley, the Incluseum "advances new ways of being a museum through critical discourse, community building and collaborative practice related to inclusion in museums" (Incluseum). This website features regular blog entries from a variety of museum professional contributors. Additionally, the Incluseum has an extensive resources page filled with articles, tools, and blog links. Among the numerous consultants available, the Inclusive Knowledge Community, and the Incluseum, you and your museum have a selection of learning tools to understand inclusion.

Begin Implementing Inclusion by Expanding Your Professional Network

In order to implement inclusion in our museums, we must gather resources to understand inclusion. We must train our personnel, our boards, and our communities to be partners in an inclusive experience. In this chapter I have outlined a broad swath of tools for inclusion, and I hope that you will use these tools to further understand the social role of the museum. In addition, I suggest that you network with museum professionals who are practicing inclusion successfully, connecting with communities and providing meaningful experiences for all.

8

Tools for Evaluating Inclusion in Your Museum

As museums grapple with their new social role and the application of inclusive practices, we will begin to see a higher demand for evaluation processes. Museum practitioners will want to know, "Is my museum inclusive?" "How can I prove my museum is inclusive?" "Is there a rubric, a metric, a standard for measuring the inclusivity of my museum?" The current answer is *no*. We have no standardized evaluation processes for inclusion in the United States. We do, however, have examples from other nations that we can draw upon to generate our standards. In particular, the EU and UK governments heavily evaluate social inclusion in museums:

> Questions regarding the definition of "value" and the measurement of the social impact of culture are relevant to museums internationally, and the way these are approached in the United Kingdom can provide museums and policy makers in other countries with an example to follow or reject. (West and Smith 2005, 275–88)

This chapter will propose a series of evaluative techniques based on social science research methods and the national standards of EU/UK policies on social inclusion. I will also suggest blended approaches, melding American sensibility with Western

European metrics. My ultimate goal is to produce a uniquely American set of tools for evaluating inclusion in our museums.

Types of Evaluation Tools

There are several main categories of evaluation techniques: quantitative, qualitative, and mixed-methods. Quantitative evaluations allow us to examine a phenomenon—in this case, inclusivity—from a numerical perspective. Quantitative assessment results in numerical data that we can interpret through mathematical means such as statistics. I should note that in the United States, statistics have received negative attention, especially in the media (Davies 2017; Rampell 2017). The distrust of statistical findings may be the result of political misuse and warping of interpretations (Davies 2017; Rampell 2017). Statistical data can be a powerful tool in creating a picture of your museum's inclusivity. Statistical findings can be interpreted and displayed visually through charts, figures, tables, and infographics. Visual representations of statistical data can be impressive and influential when presenting to stakeholders. The Center for the Future of Museums infographic in chapter 1 is so striking that numerous museum professionals have incorporated it into their conference proceedings and presentations. In this chapter, I will address how to collect, interpret, and display quantitative data about the inclusivity of your museum. I will also examine several approaches to qualitative evaluation. Qualitative evaluation allows you to explore a phenomenon from a descriptive viewpoint. Qualitative data is often subjective and verbal. For many years, qualitative data was viewed as less "scientific" than quantitative; yet it has risen in popularity in part due to its usefulness for revealing the nuances of a phenomenon (Bryman 1984, 75–92). As we begin to construct a shared vocabulary for discussing inclusion, qualitative data—steeped in natural language processes—will be invaluable. In this chapter, I will present possible qualitative evaluation techniques and the associated data collection, interpretation, and presentation of findings. Finally, I will discuss the merits of mixed-methods approaches to evaluation.

In a mixed-methods evaluative approach, you will merge quantitative statistical data with qualitative descriptive data to present a holistic view of the inclusivity of your museum. In all three types of data evaluation, I will address the creation of compelling presentations for stakeholders.

Quantitative Evaluation

It has been my experience that quantitative evaluation strategies for museums most often involve survey research. "Survey research provides a quantitative or numeric description of trends, attitudes or opinions of a population by studying a sample of that population" (Creswell 2009). Museums employ survey methods frequently, so frequently that such methods appear to lose efficacy. Whenever I mention survey methods to museum professionals, they are hesitant to be enthusiastic. I hear phrases such as "We've done surveys before—you just can't tell anything from them." I understand that museums employ survey methods but often fail to construct a useful survey instrument (construction problems), or they deploy them incorrectly (procedural issues). Many museum professionals assume that survey construction is a simple task: just ask people what you want to know. Nothing could be further from the truth, as survey construction is a nuanced process founded upon a detailed review of relevant literature. Yes, to craft the survey you want, you will first need to read. Study articles, books, blogs, and other museums with similar scenarios. Second, and this is where most museum professionals fall flat, study how to build a survey: What language? What type of questions? How to order items? In my opinion, a good survey should scaffold much like lesson plans or public speech. Don't want to waste time studying survey construction? Try to remember that you have spent countless hours as a professional studying exhibit design or conservation methods. You must also take time to consider how to evaluate your work and how to understand the evaluations of your work made by your public. In this section, I will outline some evaluation basics, but I urge you to continue your learning through the resources listed at the end of this book.

Quantitative Evaluation: Survey Creation Basics

Step 1: Consider the type of data that will most help you and your museum. It may seem simplistic, but data collection instruments—surveys—gather data. And you, as the survey designer, can shape the format of that data through initial considerations of survey construction. Do you want to know demographic information about your museum visitors? For example, do you want to know their age? It may seem like a strange place to begin—the result—but it is also the most rational point.

Second, consider the complexity of the data desired. The novice survey builder will design a survey unaware that the ten questions asked will yield data with hundreds of facets (see table 8.1).

As a general rule, the more questions you ask, the more complicated your data. Or, more accurately, the more facets to each of your questions, the more complex your data will be.

Note the complexity that results from a single question with multiple possible answers, as seen in figure 8.1: "What words would you use to describe the term *empathy*? Choose all that apply." When you consider that you may be doing analysis of

Table 8.1. Common Survey Question Types

Survey Question Type	Example Question	Example Answer	Data Yielded
Dichotomous	In the past year have you visited a museum or gallery? Yes or No	Yes	Nominal
Categorical Multiple Choice	How did you arrive at the museum today? a) Car b) Bus c) Walk	b) Car	Nominal
Interval & Likert Scale	Rate your level of agreement with the following statement: Museums should take an active role in community events. a) Completely agree b) Agree c) Neither agree nor disagree d) Disagree e) Completely disagree	b) Agree	Ordinal

One simple question yields many variations of responses from 1000 individuals

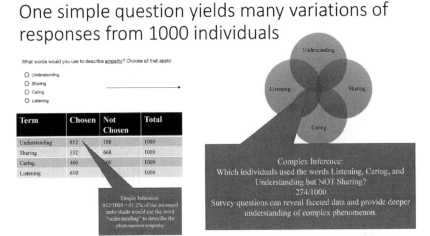

What words would you use to describe *empathy*? Choose all that apply:

○ Understanding
○ Sharing
○ Caring
○ Listening

Term	Chosen	Not Chosen	Total
Understanding	812	188	1000
Sharing	332	668	1000
Caring	400	00	1000
Listening	610		1000

Simple Inference:
812/1000 = 81.2% of the surveyed individuals would use the word "understanding" to describe the phenomenon empathy

Complex Inference:
Which individuals used the words Listening, Caring, and Understanding but NOT Sharing?
274/1000
Survey questions can reveal faceted data and provide deeper understanding of complex phenomenon.

Figure 8.1. Sample Survey Data.
Created by Laura-Edythe Coleman.

more than one variable at a time, the complexity of your findings grows exponentially. There are two main types of questions: open-ended and closed-ended. Open-ended questions are particularly useful in qualitative interviewing, as they allow the interviewee to answer in their own words. The majority of questions that you will use in a survey instrument are closed-ended: questions for which your respondent must select among the answer choices. As the creator of the survey, you decide what the answer choices will be for each question.

Third, scaffold your questionnaire. I always start with easier concrete questions and work toward more difficult abstract notions. Scaffolding is essential, as the length of survey questionnaires matters. As you prepare a survey, you may have twenty questions you want answers to. But your average respondent may not have that much time or energy to devote to answering your questions. Here we encounter the concept of *survey fatigue*. Just as we have the accepted idea of museum fatigue, there is also survey fatigue: a point at which your respondent tires of answering questions and will stop answering thoughtfully or cease answering altogether. A well-constructed survey rarely takes a respondent to this point of exhaustion.

Fourth, by the time you are creating a survey instrument, you should have a strong notion of who your population is. Surveys are intended to yield data that is representative of the total population of interest, and therefore survey findings become generalizable to that population. Do not create a survey in the hope of learning the demographics of your community. Why? Because we have census data for that! There are many sources of good community demographic data. Specific sources of demographic data are listed in the resources section of this book. Should you ask for demographic data from each respondent? Definitely! But you do not ask to determine the demographics of the community. If you collect demographic data from each respondent, you will be able to verify whether the group of people you surveyed (your sample) is representative of the community population.

Fifth, in constructing the actual language of your survey questions, please be mindful of your language. I am referring to more than the necessity of translations into alternative languages, such as Spanish, Creole, or Braille; I am urging you to write surveys in a way that is easily understood. For example, I often use a sixth-grade reading level to guide my vocabulary choices in writing question text. Refrain from using museum jargon. It is tempting to use terminology that you are familiar with in your survey, but remember that you want to know what your community thinks—not whether they can parrot you!

Pilot Testing

The last step of survey construction is an iterative one: the pilot test. Once you have written your questions, test your survey: first on your museum colleagues, then with individuals outside the museum field. Look for signs of confusion: Do test respondents reread questions? Do they ask for clarification or terminology to be defined? Do they sigh or seem tired after several questions? Shrugging? After they complete your survey, ask for feedback. The first questions I ask are "What do you think this survey was about? What was easy to understand? Which questions seemed unclear?" Note that I never use the phrase *too hard* or *too difficult* because I have found that it makes my pilot testers feel unintelligent. Take the suggestions your pilot testers give you, and polish the wording of your survey. This final step of survey construction is time-consuming but well worth the effort.

Quantitative Evaluation: Survey Deployment Basics

After you have a polished survey instrument available, you must now begin the act of surveying people. If you do not deploy your survey correctly, all those hours of survey construction are in vain. Before you engage even one docent to stand around with a clipboard, you must develop a procedure for deploying your survey.

First, decide on how you will choose people to survey. Most museums make the mistake of sampling only the individuals who come through their doors. In social science research, this form of survey sampling is a convenience sample. Convenience sampling is nonrandom and not useful for making generalizations about the general population. Sometimes the notion of random is confusing, and museum practitioners will ask, "But aren't we randomly selecting if we survey every third person who walks through our doors?" The answer is "sorry, not really." Why? The selected sample is from a predetermined group: individuals who decided to attend the museum that day. As we know from other research such as that done by the Center for the Future of Museums, the group of people who attend museums does not reflect or resemble the population of our communities (Center for the Future of Museums 2015). If you only want to know about the people who visit your museum already, then your population is museum attendees. If, however, you want to know about your museum's societal impact, then you must sample more widely by sampling society. But how will you sample your community? Despite the inherent differences between communities, and although each museum is unique, you will sample your community using similar (if not identical) social science methods to the ones outlined in this book. Before you assume that a random sample of your community is impossible, let us look at an early successful American example. In

1983, researcher Marilyn Hood led a team of thirty-five museum volunteers to randomly survey the population of Toledo (rural, urban, suburban) (Hood 1983, 50–57). The museum gained valuable insight into the motivations of visitors and nonvisitors in its community. Hood's findings helped the Toledo museum identify the ways in which it was not meeting community needs (Hood 1983, 50–57). Surely if Hood could survey the Toledo community over the course of three weeks in the spring of 1983, then you should be able to reach a representative sample of your community. Seriously? Yes. Remember, you do not have to ask everyone in your community; you need only obtain a representative sample of your community. Hood was able to draw substantial conclusions about the Toledo community based upon telephone surveys of only 502 respondents (Hood 1983, 50–57). As a museum professional poised to perform surveying in the twenty-first century, you have tools—including online ones—for reaching your community. Leverage technology and social media, or even go door-to-door. An afternoon of careful surveying, canvassing your neighborhoods, can yield a mountain of invaluable data. How many people should you survey? The higher the number of respondents, the higher your confidence level: the statistic that expresses the accuracy of the degree to which our sample matches the population (Babbie 2009). For more information on sampling and surveying tools, please see the resources section of this book.

Second, once you have identified your survey respondents or the quota of respondents needed, develop an exact procedure for connecting with these individuals. Write it down. A simple set of instructions and an explanatory paragraph is read either by the respondents (self-administration of a survey) or to the respondents by the surveyor. This text sets the stage for better data collection and often doubles as the moment to obtain respondent permission. Please note that although not every institution will require that you obtain an individual's permission to administer a survey, I think it is a vital aspect of respect. To learn more about the ethical conduct of research and administering surveys, see the resources section of this book. Remember that a good introduction and salutation sets the tone for a respectful relationship with your community. In practicing survey administration (and I do suggest that you practice!), make sure to greet and thank respondents individually.

Quantitative Evaluation: Data Analysis and Findings Presentation

Quantitative analysis is the "numerical representation and manipulation of observations for the purposes of describing and explaining the phenomena that those observations reflect" (Babbie 2009). The majority of quantitative data analysis is performed through computer software such as SPSS (Babbie 2009). Regardless of the type of software that you use, your first step in quantitative data analysis is to create a codebook (Babbie 2009). A codebook allows you, the human, to assign meaning to the computer-generated values in an analysis. For instance, if you have the survey question "How often to do you attend the X museum?" and this question has five possible answers ("never," "rarely," "occasionally," "frequently," "always"), you would encode these in a numerical way; in essence, translate the answers into machine-readable information. My codebook would look like table 8.2.

The first analysis I perform is a univariate analysis. I look at each variable individually and examine the descriptive frequencies. I look at measures of central tendency: mean, median, and

Table 8.2. Codebook Example

Question: How often do you attend the X museum?

Term	Definition	Computer Code
"never"	Respondent has never attended the X museum.	0
"rarely"	Respondent has attended the X museum once.	1
"occasionally"	Respondent has attended the X museum 1–3 times previously.	2
"frequently"	Respondent has attended the X museum more than once in the past year.	3
"always"	Respondent attends the X museum on a regular basis.	4

mode. After I have looked at each variable individually, I then study variable combinations: bivariate and multivariate. This is only the beginning of the many statistical tests that can be run once your data is appropriately coded. Although a complete description of the possible statistical tests is beyond the scope of this text, I encourage you to seek out resources to understand the data that you collect.

Once you have analyzed your quantitative data, take time to interpret your results. Find another museum professional to look over your results. Do they come to the same conclusions? There are multiple procedures available for ensuring reliability and validity of your research, and I suggest that at a minimum you enlist the help of another individual to check your codes. When you are reasonably confident of your findings, consider which of your results will be most important to your stakeholders. I have found that stakeholders benefit from a balanced mix of visual aids and explanatory text. Place charts, graphs, figures, and tables inline next to the explanatory text, not tucked away in the indices of your report (Babbie 2009).

You can implement other types of quantitative data collection in your museum. Surveys are considered obtrusive in nature, but different data-collection processes such as observation are less so. These unobtrusive methods research behavior without affecting it (Babbie 2009). For example, Webb et al. found discreet ways of determining the popularity of exhibits in 1966 by measuring, quantitatively, the wear and tear on the floor in front of exhibit cases (Babbie 2009). Your museum can also engage in quantitative data analysis of previously collected data. What collected data? Museum visitor numbers, ticket sales, and website analytics, to name a few.

Qualitative Evaluation

The nuances of individual museums simply cannot be captured by a quantitative study. The impact museums have upon their communities cannot be described in mere numbers and statistics. Qualitative research study is defined by Creswell as "a means for exploring and understanding the meaning individuals or groups ascribe to a social or human problem" (Creswell 2009). Your museum may benefit from several of the popular qualitative methodologies: interviews, focus groups, and case studies. I encourage museums to embark upon qualitative research frequently, as such studies are often characterized by a desire to "empower individuals to share their stories, hear their voices" (Creswell 2013). I prefer intensive interviewing to focus groups, as I learn more by listening to the uninterrupted thoughts of another person. I have also found that interviewees are more comfortable engaging in sensitive conversations when in a one-on-one scenario. In this section I will describe the basic steps for performing an intensive interview with a respondent.

Intensive or in-depth interviewing is conducted to learn the stories and histories of individuals, sometimes with the desire to glean insight on a specific phenomenon. Seidman (1998) draws from Vygotsky to succinctly state, "Every word that people use in telling their stories is a microcosm of their consciousness" (Seidman 1998). You, too, can learn from every word spoken by your respondents.

Interviewing is a mode of inquiry that does not attempt to find definitive answers to questions, and it is not chosen as a primary format for testing hypotheses in research (Seidman 1998). Interviewing is, however, a research arrangement for understanding the experiences of individuals and the making of meaning within a dialogue relationship. Interviewing is more than a research format: it is a performative relationship that exists between interviewer and respondent. Miller and Crabtree define interviewing as a "research-gathering approach that seeks to create a listening space where meaning is constructed through an interexchange/co-creation of verbal viewpoints in the interest of scientific knowing" (Miller and Crabtree 2004). In my interviewing, I pose open-ended verbal questions targeted to jointly explore a specific individual and their story. I am committed to the usage of a dialectic approach to create a space for dialogue and the construction of meaning with each of the interview participants. You, too, can leverage interviewing strategies for understanding, on a descriptive level, the community around your museum.

Qualitative Evaluation: Setting the Stage for Interviewing

Interviewing is commonly misunderstood to be a simple format for communication. It is in fact a complicated process that
requires forethought and careful planning. At first glance, an
interview appears to be a casual event, one in which questions
and answers are given and received in a dialogue. As a trained
interviewer, I am aware that my skills are far from casual. I plan
my interview encounter, from start to finish: I plan the location,
the recording tools, the questions I will ask, and the scripted text
that I will use. My preferred format is semistructured—I use a
list of predetermined open-ended questions with each of my
interviewees, but I allow them to answer the questions in their
own way. I am constantly aware of my surroundings, my participant, and regularly check my own emotional state as I listen.
I recommend recording interviews on paper and/or on audio/
video devices. How many interviews should you perform? I
suggest you work until the point of *saturation*: the moment when
you are no longer learning new information by performing additional interviews. Quite frankly, no one can tell you when that
moment of saturation will occur—it simply will. There are several formats available for interviewing individually or in focus
groups, and I encourage you to check the resources in the back
of this book for more information. No matter the type of qualitative interview you choose to perform, I highly recommend that
you spend ample time transcribing your conversations. Many a
researcher has spent countless hours arranging for and performing interviews only to fail in this important step of transcription.
Do not rely on your feelings concerning the interviews; transcribe
the words, as they will be the basis of the language you can use
to describe the phenomenon of inclusion.

Qualitative Evaluation: Data Analysis and Presentation of Interviews

After you have transcribed your interviews and notes, spend time
developing a codebook. Unsure of where to start your codes? I
use the qualitative data analysis software NVivo, based upon the
idea of NVivo coding process. I filter through the text of my in-

terviews, looking for the use of terminology. In particular, when I have researched museum inclusivity, I have combed through the text to find words that my respondents use to describe inclusion. The language used by my interviewees often surprises me, and each interview session yields new lines of inquiry. Take time to analyze how frequently your interviewees use words of interest such as *diversity, inclusion, accessibility,* and *welcoming*. Work diligently to organize the words used with Post-it notes, dry-erase boards, or mindmaps. If you have indeed performed interviews until the point of saturation, you should be able to develop terminology and conclusions about the views of your community.

Unlike quantitative data, your interview data will not yield numbers and statistics (other than frequency of word use). Instead, look for the association of words within the text: Do interviewees equate one term with another? Do they use one word to define another concept? These relationships in language are important. Presentations of qualitative data should include poignant quotes and relevant anecdotes. Remember not to change or "clean up" the language of your interviewees—their voices matter, and the ways in which they talk and their accent are important to conveying meaning. If I include an image in my presentations of qualitative interviews, I will use a picture from the museum or the collection. I never use a picture of my interviewees in my presentations; instead, I display their quotes—most often anonymized.

Qualitative Evaluation: A Word about Ethical Conduct

Qualitative research is intensely personal. You are asking individuals to speak candidly about their views and lived experiences. The interview design phase must also include the writing of an informed consent document. In this document, you should clearly outline for your interviewees the purpose of the research study and the time commitment expected from the respondent, as well as the risks and benefits of participation. Informed written consent should be complemented by the use of verbal assent. At the beginning of each interview session, please inform your interviewee again of the risks and benefits of participation and ask them to verbally agree to the interview for the recording. At all times, respect the individual that you interview. You may not agree with what they say about your museum or about local history, but none of that matters—they are giving you their time and energy, and you must respect them. Always introduce and thank your interviewees by name, and be prepared to stop the interview process at any time of your interviewee's choosing— even if you are not done asking questions!

Mixed-Method Evaluation: A Powerful Combination

My goal in this chapter is to convey that "no one metric or powerful story is sufficient enough to characterize a museum's public value contributions. A complete convincing evaluation requires an array of evidence that when tied together, provides an authentic picture of the institution and its effects" (Scott 2013). Yes, I advocate for the use of "mixed-methods" evaluation strategies: quantitative and qualitative methodologies used in tandem to explore a phenomenon. Why am I so convinced that mixed-methods research is the best strategy for studying inclusion? Inclusion addresses the multidimensional social problems of exclusion. We cannot understand our economic impact upon a community without numerical data (quantitative), and we cannot fathom the impact of economic problems without descriptive data (qualitative). How do we mix methods? We can use quantitative and qualitative evaluation in different combinations. I prefer to use a quantitative method (surveying) to inform in a sequential manner a qualitative method (interviewing) (Creswell 2009). I perfect my interview questions based upon answers to my survey questions. To learn more about combining methods to create powerful museum studies, see the list in the resources section of this book.

Examples of Evaluation Techniques

In this section, I will outline two types of evaluation techniques used in recent years within the United Kingdom, Australia, and European Union. I have divided these studies according to the population that was examined in the hope that it will shape the way in which you identify the proper techniques for understanding your community. First are examples of quantitative evaluation of inclusive museum practice. Second is an example of qualitative evaluation of inclusive museum practice.

Quantitative Evaluation Examples

Governments in Western Europe and the United Kingdom have required quantitative evaluations of museum inclusivity since the turn of the twenty-first century. Policymakers in these nations have officially linked inclusion with cultural institutions (European Union 2005). Significant national surveys have been conducted on an annual basis of the households in the United Kingdom; this is in addition to routinely performed census data of the entire population. The Focus on Cultural Diversity survey provides a "historic baseline in terms of attendance, participation, and attitude" (Oakley and Naylor 2005). This survey was administered to 7,600 UK residents in 2003 (Oakley and Naylor 2005). The UK government has amassed both demographic data on its populations and the frequency of museum attendance by its people. As this data has been collected annually for decades, the aggregated data sets provide an excellent baseline and indicators for monitoring societal trends in the United Kingdom. Other nations have followed the UK example and initiated surveys concerning inclusion.

Example: Northern Adelaide Social Inclusion Survey (NASIS 2005)

The Australian government developed and implemented the NASIS 2005 to generate data concerning an impoverished area of Australia: Northern Adelaide. The survey was created as a "model that provides a range of indicators of social inclusion and exclusion that enables the measurement of change over time" (Spoehr 2007). Although not specifically a museum-related survey, this survey could be adapted as a measurement instrument for inclusion in the United States.

Analyzing and Measuring Social Inclusion in a Global Context

The majority of social inclusion instruments and indicators have been developed as a result of adaptions to the Social Capital Integrated Questionnaire (SCIQ). Developed for the World Bank, the International Bank for Reconstruction and Development, this questionnaire reflects a commitment to examine the multidimensional nature of poverty. As an attempt to measure ·social capital, conceptually this survey draws upon the work of Bourdieau and combines the two widely accepted concepts of social capital: social capital as resources available to individuals as promoted by Burt, Lin, and Portes; and social capital as a reflection of collective community health as explored by Putnam (Wilson 2006, 335–60).

Intentionally multidimensional in its approach, this questionnaire explores the networks within communities, the "respondents' subjective perceptions of the trustworthiness of other people and key institutions that shape their lives, as well as the norms of cooperation and reciprocity that surround attempts to work together to solve problems" (Grootaert et al. 2004). Although the authors of this questionnaire do not purport it to be exhaustive, it is extensive in scope. Items are arranged into categories: "groups and networks; trust and solidarity; collective action and cooperation; information and communication; social cohesion and inclusion; empowerment and political action" (Grootaert et al. 2004). These questions inquire into the nucleus of social capital and inclusion, and they are intended to be part of a greater research project.

Developed, tested, and adapted for different studies, the SCIQ has achieved recognition as being a reliable and valid instrument (Grootaert et al. 2004). The unit of measurement involved in the SCIQ is the individual or household, the intention being that the aggregation of multiple individuals or households will create a community-wide snapshot of social capital and inclusion. A significant benefit of this questionnaire is that while it does provide a community Polaroid, it also may be used in a longitudinal study and repeated, thus exponentially increasing the significance of its findings. To learn more about the SCIQ, how to adapt it for your community, and to explore the various questions related to social inclusion, please see the resources section of this book.

Qualitative Evaluation Examples

The examples in this section illustrate the necessity for qualitative evaluation of the social role of our museums:

> While quantification is essential for analysing poverty and social exclusion, quantitative indicators are still not sufficient. These need to be accompanied by qualitative evidence, which helps interpret the numbers and provides a start in understanding the underlying mechanisms. Significant elements of human experience cannot readily be reduced to a simple scale. Findings from qualitative studies can provide some reassurance that quantitative indicators correspond to the reality on the ground. (Atkinson and United Nations 2010)

Museum research literature contains multiple examples of qualitative evaluation. This is particularly the case in the United Kingdom, where qualitative evaluations have been conducted concerning the socially inclusive role of the museum. In 1999 to 2000, professors Eilean Hooper-Greenhill, Richard Sandell, Theano Moussouri, and Helen O'Riain led a team of researchers to study twenty-two UK museums, resulting in the GLLAM report (Group for Large Local Authority Museums 2000, 1–59). Through open and exploratory methods of qualitative interviews, the researchers discovered that "the lack of policies and support" contributed to an "invisibility of the work being done" by museum professionals (Group for Large Local Authority Museums 2000, 1–59). The GLLAM report indicated that the term *social inclusion* was ambiguous at best. This finding was echoed by the research of Tlili (2008), in which "diverse terminology" was revealed during the qualitative interviews (Tlili 2008, 123–47).

The Research Centre for Museums and Galleries (RCMG) in the Department of Museum Studies at the University of Leicester is responsible for several qualitative evaluations of the socially inclusive role of museums. In 2001, researchers Jocelyn Dodd and Helen O'Riain performed interviews with museum staff and community members concerning the Open Museum (Dodd et al. 2002). Their research found that "participants interviewed as part of this study clearly illustrate the profound significance the Open Museum has had on their lives."

The use of qualitative methods provided the researchers with rich quotes, such as "I've learnt how to express myself in different forms of art. . . . It was a huge change in my life. I was able to express myself for the first time" (Dodd et al. 2002). Detailed and subjective quotes such as the ones outlined in the Open Museum report would not have been made possible through the use of quantitative instruments. There are significant advantages to performing qualitative research: original verbiage is kept intact; relationships between terms and concepts are explained; and stories bring to life quantitative data.

Beginnings of Evaluation Strategies for the United States

The field of museum evaluation—especially for understanding societal impact—has not yet solidified into discrete scientific measurements. In particular, evaluations must "extend beyond the views of visitors and museum members and involve other stakeholders and citizens, including those who do not use the museum" (Mary Ellen Munley, in Scott 2013). We can build upon the research performed by our UK counterparts, but we must be "successful in demonstrating the importance of its mission and work to the overall quality of life of the community" (Munley, in Scott 2013). The work of Carol Scott in the evaluation of the public value of museums is a good starting point for any institution seeking to understand its impact upon a community. Although her work, *Museums and Public Value: Creating Sustainable Futures*, is not specifically written to assess inclusivity, chapter 4 by Mary Ellen Munley is particularly applicable to performing evaluations of inclusion.

Using Evaluation Results to Convince Stakeholders

At this point, you probably realize the benefits of inclusion for your museum and your community. Yet you still must convince your stakeholders of the value that you offer to your community. From beginning to end of any exhibit or program you will need to evaluate the impact your museum has on inclusion. How will you explain your choices to your stakeholders? First, remember, "no one metric or powerful story is sufficient to characterize a museum's public value contributions" (Munley, in Scott 2013). You should not rely on only one type of measurement, data, or anecdote to convey the success of your museum.

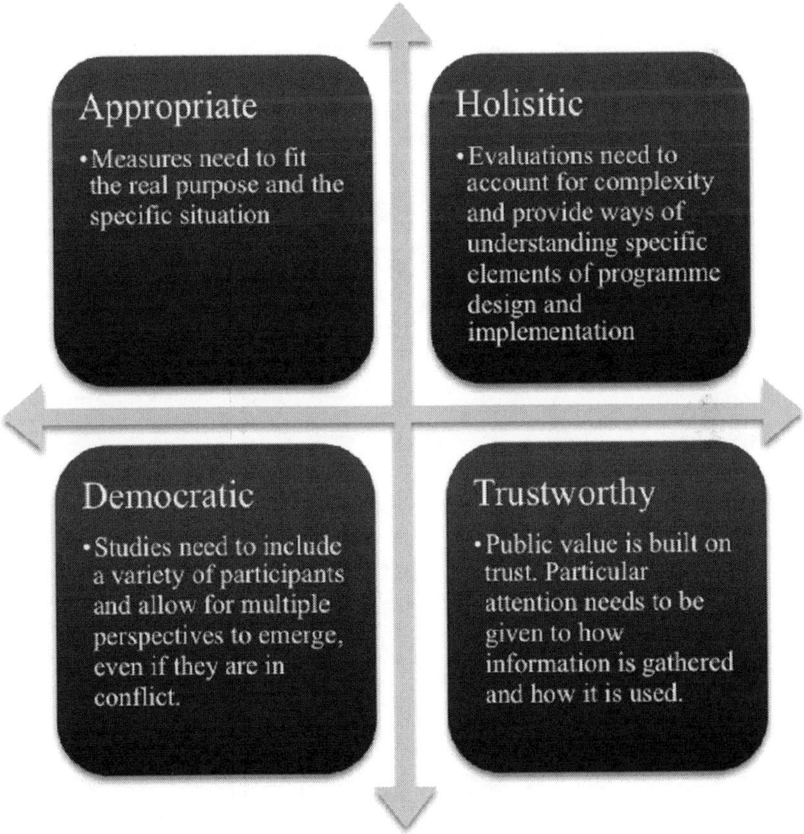

Appropriate
• Measures need to fit the real purpose and the specific situation

Holisitic
• Evaluations need to account for complexity and provide ways of understanding specific elements of programme design and implementation

Democratic
• Studies need to include a variety of participants and allow for multiple perspectives to emerge, even if they are in conflict.

Trustworthy
• Public value is built on trust. Particular attention needs to be given to how information is gathered and how it is used.

Figure 8.2. Munley's Methods and Measures.
Created by Laura-Edythe Coleman, derived from Mary Ellen Munley in Scott 2013.

According to Munley, "a complete, convincing evaluation requires an array of evidence that, when tied together, provides an authentic picture of the institution and its effects" (see table 8.2; Munley, in Scott 2013).

Articulating the Social Role of Museums

American museums, like Western European and UK museums, need to prove that their practices are becoming more inclusive. It is only a matter of time before policymakers and other stakeholders in the United States follow their EU and UK counterparts and demand that museums prove their inclusive role in order to continue to receive funding. Museum professionals must become adept not only at what they do in a museum but also in communicating that role to others. A necessary step for museum professionals is to learn how to perform evaluations upon their work. A cautionary tale has been told from the 2000 GLLAM report in the United Kingdom (in which museums collected data concerning inclusive practice) that "the data was rarely analysed and the findings were not always summarized and presented in a report" (Group for Large Local Authority Museums 2000, 1–59). As American museum professionals learn new evaluation strategies and techniques, care must be taken to follow through with an intended goal of such studies: *to articulate value*. The GLLAM report found that "overall, evaluation processes are poorly understood and haphazardly carried out. Summative data is not related to base-line data and so change in knowledge, skills or attitude cannot be demonstrated. Evidence cannot be provided for social outcomes" (Group for Large Local Authority Museums 2000, 1–59). American museums, and the professionals who work within, must be vigilant in articulating our social role, lest we find ourselves surrounded by data and little funding.

9

Advocates, Agents, and Architects of Inclusion for American Museums

There can be little doubt that the American museum profession is changing, that it has changed, and will continue to evolve as museums adapt themselves to the needs of society. In this book, we have discussed the theoretical and historical underpinnings of inclusion, the types of inclusion for museums, and the tools for implementing and evaluating inclusive practices. In this chapter, I will highlight several of those individuals who are acting as advocates of inclusion, being agents of inclusive practice, and designing the architecture of inclusion for American museums. I outline a spectrum of participation, in which many individuals are advocates for inclusive practices. Some are also agents of social change, and only a few are true architects of inclusion for American museums (see figure 9.1). As you will note, the divisions between these three categories—advocates, agents, and architects—are blurred. I have intentionally created a messy figure to display the fact that individuals often cross from one role to another as needed. Each of the individuals I will mention brings a unique set of skills and experiences to bear on increasing inclusion within our museums. In this chapter, I unashamedly promote the work of my colleagues: museum professionals, academics, bloggers, consultants, and social justice advocates who further the cause of inclusion for American museums.

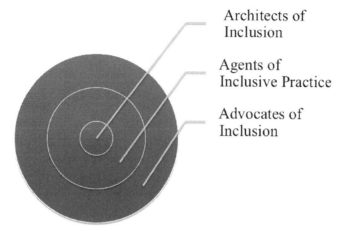

Architects of
Inclusion

Agents of
Inclusive Practice

Advocates of
Inclusion

Figure 9.1. Advocates, Agents, and Architects of Inclusion.
Created by Laura-Edythe Coleman.

I highlight these individuals because their work has been instrumental in promoting inclusion for American museums.

Advocates of Inclusion

An increasing number of American museum professionals, volunteers, and academics are vocal about creating inclusion within American museums. The many individuals who are speaking about inclusion vary in degree of passion, articulation, and perspective. In this section, I have included an array of persons, all of whom are committed to expanding the social role of museums. These individuals leverage media through talks, text, and Twitter to advocate inclusive practices for museums. I chose these people because they refuse to be silent, and they continue to speak out for the implementation of inclusion.

Rose Paquet Kinsley and Aletheia Wittman

Rose and Aletheia are co-founders of the website Incluseum.com. Since 2012, they have blogged about the social role of museums, especially as it pertains to inclusion. While not intentionally an "American" focused blog, the contributors tend to speak from an

American perspective. Rose is currently a doctoral candidate in Information Science at the University of Washington iSchool, and Aletheia is a collections interpreter for the Burke Museum of Natural History and Culture in Seattle, Washington. Rose and Aletheia envisioned the Incluseum as more than a mere website, and they describe their work as "a project based in Seattle, Washington that advances new ways of being a museum through critical discourse, community building and collaborative practice related to inclusion in museums" (Incluseum 2015). These founders advocate for and work to create informal partnerships between museum professionals to foster inclusive practices. On defining inclusion, Rose says that "inclusion is radical, it's more than just a policy that comes from the state or institutions, it's about shifting how I on an individual level see the problems" (Coleman et al. 2016). Rose and Aletheia are not the sole contributors to Incluseum.com; a variety of museum professionals contributes much of the content. The Incluseum is no ordinary website: it is a knowledge community that is a *model of organizational inclusion*. Both of the founders see themselves as facilitators of a critical dialogue who bring people together to "build bridges" (Coleman et al. 2016). Several of the inclusion advocates in this chapter first appeared to the public online community as guest bloggers on Incluseum.com. Overall, Rose and Aletheia have "linked inclusion with greater structures like oppression, systems of racism and sexism—the oppression that functions on an everyday basis" (Coleman et al. 2016). Both Rose and Aletheia present in museum conferences, write articles, and advocate across social media for inclusion. Most recently, Rose and Aletheia have served as project advisors to Museum as Site for Social Action (MASS Action), an initiative of the Minnesota Institute of Art to increase social justice dialogue through museums. In addition to the website, Aletheia often speaks out on Twitter and can be followed @AletheiaJane. Her work through the Incluseum reflects her commitment to the "work to be done in the US" (Coleman et al. 2016).

nikhil trivedi

nikhil trivedi is an applications web developer for the Art Institute of Chicago and social justice advocate for museums. His work, while primarily social justice oriented, demonstrates his capacity to advocate for inclusive practices in museums. nikhil is well known for his 2015 Museum Computing Network presentation, an "Anti-Oppression Manifesto," in which he declared that "we fight for a more just world, we work to heal our communities from historic traumatic events that are still alive for many of us today, we work to distribute power more equitably and to make our world safer for those that are the most unsafe" (trivedi 2015). nikhil, like many of the advocates in this chapter, is not paid to increase awareness around inclusive practices, and he summarizes his work like this:

> I live two lives. At the Art Institute of Chicago for 10 years I've been surrounded by technical innovators . . . outside of work, I'm surrounded by innovators of a different sort—grassroots community organizers, queer activists, radical philanthropists, prison abolitionists, rape victim advocates, healers and artists, all who look at the world through an anti-oppression lens. (trivedi 2015)

nikhil is outspoken concerning social justice advocacy. However, I would like to shed light on his lesser-known work, "Take 5 Minutes at the Beginning of a Design Phase to Consider How to Make Your Project Anti-Oppressive." His writings are available from GitHub, not a traditional blogging platform but a code repository service (see figure 9.2). Although he wrote these documents to combat oppression, many of his suggestions would easily fit an application for inclusive museum practices—particularly digital inclusion. Whether online at GitHub, on Twitter @nikhiltri, or in person at museum conferences, nikhil continues to call upon "museum professionals to recognize their role, as institutions, in systemic oppression." He most recently served as a project advisor to MASS Action.

Adrianne Russell and Aleia Brown

Russell and Brown are best known for their founding of the Twitter hashtag #museumsrespondtoferguson, a social justice advocacy movement among museum professionals. Adrianne

Russell is a self-proclaimed "museum evangelist" and advocate for inclusion in museums. In her daily work, she is a museum and nonprofit consultant, and she recently contributed to the toolkit created by MASS Action. She has been featured on the Incluseum and has an online platform, "Cabinet of Curiosities," located within her website: adriannerussell.wordpress.com. Adrianne has been active both online and in person at museum conferences. She encourages museums to join the fight for social justice and for the adoption of inclusive practices. Aleia Brown "holds a joint appointment at the Michigan State University Museum and the Department of History" (Fletcher 2016). As advocates, Russell and Brown want "museum professionals to understand that they are not alone in their pursuit towards more inclusive spaces" (Fletcher 2016). They offer insight into the impact that their work has had through Twitter:

> The hashtag is responsible for starting and continuing the most public conversation on race and intersectionality in museum studies. In terms of ideological shifts, museum staff have to change the way they talk about identity. The conversations are often muddled with phrases like, "these issues" and "difficult histories." Sometimes in chats and consultation groups, we have banned those phrases to force people to clarify what is troubling them. (Fletcher 2016)

Russell and Brown continue to advocate across social media for a more just society through museums: "Much of our future work will occur outside of museums and we are proud of that. We love museums and their potential, which is why we are so dedicated to making them better. We are glad to be part of a tradition of black women working outside of institutions to encourage fundamental changes within institutions" (Fletcher 2016). Russell and Brown are not alone in their work; many have joined their efforts to promote change within museums. It is important to note that Russell and Brown are working from outside the museum inward, and such a pathway for social change is a "tradition of black women." As museum professionals, we are aware of the lack of ethnic diversity among museum professionals, especially in leadership (Schonfeld, Westermann, and Sweeney 2015).

Nicole Ivy

The American Alliance of Museums is seeking to understand and implement inclusion across the field. In 2017, Nicole Ivy became the American Alliance of Museums' first director of inclusion. Dr. Ivy leads the "Alliance's strategic initiatives around diversity, equity, accessibility, and inclusion." She is also an advocate for inclusion online via Twitter @nicotron3000.

Porchia Moore

Dr. Porchia Moore is an advocate of inclusion online via Twitter @PorchiaMuseM, through multiple projects such as MASS Action, Visitors of Color (co-created with nikhil trivedi), and Museum Hue. The Visitors of Color project has a mission statement that clearly outlines the social role of museums. "Our passion is museums, our focus is people, our position is intersectionality" (Moore and trivedi). Through the Visitors of Color project, Dr. Moore and nikhil trivedi crafted "The Visitors of Color Guide to Resistance" (Moore and trivedi). Dr. Moore has been featured as a regular contributor to the Incluseum and is well known for her talk "The Danger of the D Word" (Moore 2014).

Dina Bailey

Dina Bailey is the CEO of Mountain Top Vision consulting and an adjunct instructor at Johns Hopkins University. She has previously worked with the National Center for Civil and Human Rights in Atlanta, Georgia, and the National Underground Railroad Freedom Center in Cincinnati, Ohio. Dina is an advocate for inclusion online via Twitter @DinaABailey. Most recently, Dina facilitated a dialogue at the 2017 American Alliance of Museum's conference. At this conference, she displayed her ability to successfully address a highly charged discussion concerning race and oppression: "While I do not make light of the turning point, my role in it, or the productive dialogue that followed, my focus was (and continues to be) on how and why it ended more successfully than it started" (Bailey 2017). Her advocacy efforts have

Figure 9.2.   Advocate as Ambassador: Dina Bailey.
Image courtesy of Juliee Becker 2017.

demonstrated her strong awareness of the fact that "some museum professionals are well-versed in topics and themes related to equity and inclusion, while others have not engaged deeply, or perhaps have even avoided, such issues" (Bailey 2017). Most recently, she contributed to the toolkit of MASS Action.

Agents of Inclusive Practice

Increasing numbers of advocates are putting their words into action and becoming agents of inclusive practice. I suspect that there exists a greater number of museum professionals engaging their communities as agents of inclusion than is reported. In particular, museum professionals may be acting as agents of inclusion without simultaneously advocating for inclusion via social media. I have not included the many "silent" workers who may exist in our museums, as I have little way to report their views if they do not proclaim them publicly. I do, however, want to explicitly state that this section, "Agents of Inclusive Practice," is missing those silent workers. Below I have outlined several examples of museum professionals acting as advocates for inclusion and agents of inclusive practice within their museums.

Kate Livingston

Kate Livingston is a self-proclaimed "activator, a creative, a facilitator, a strategist, and a change agent." Kate advocates online via Twitter, @exposyourmuseum, for inclusive museum practice and appears in person at museum conferences. She has used her rigorous background in research methods to create theoretically based inclusive solutions for museums: "From comprehensive evaluation to participatory staff training and group facilitation, I will craft a customized plan to ensure you achieve your goals." Her work encompasses several aspects of museum practice, of which inclusion is significant, and her latest projects can be viewed online at www.exposeyourmuseum.com.

Gretchen Jennings

Gretchen Jennings is most well known for her work on institutional empathy practices. She advocates online via Twitter, @empatheticmuse, for museums to become more intentional in their social role. While she advocates for empathy, her advocacy work often aligns with the promotion of inclusion practices for museums. She has been featured on the Incluseum and also has her website, empatheticmuseum.com, a digital space for promoting her Museum Maturity Model. She recently contributed to MASS Action's toolkit publication.

Kayleigh Bryant-Greenwell

Kayleigh Bryant-Greenwell is education specialist at the National Museum of African American History and Culture in Washington, DC. She is both an advocate for inclusion and an agent of inclusionary practices. As an advocate, she speaks out online via Twitter, @KayleighbinDC, and through her website, curatorally.com. She describes her advocacy thusly:

"As advocate for social justice/activism within museum practice and an avid disruptor of status quo, I share my insights towards reshaping the museum through amplifying and nurturing community agency at conferences and the occasional blog" (Bryant-Greenwell 2014). She also recently contributed to the toolkit by MASS Action. Kayleigh's work extends beyond advocacy; she is also an agent of inclusionary practices through her programs: *A Seat at the Table* and *Women, Arts, and Social Change*. In particular, *A Seat at the Table* "provides a platform to consider the challenges faced by African Americans towards inclusion and citizenship and aims to play a key role to personal and societal betterment, aspiring to jumpstart critical thinking skills and creativity through curated activities designed for exchanging ideas and strategizing for a better world" (Bryant-Greenwell 2017). She describes her public programs as "participatory ways to engage audiences with the museum, through advancing social consciousness, activism, creativity and critical thinking" (Bryant-Greenwell 2015). Kayleigh's work meets the criteria for promotion of first-tier inclusion: personal, participatory, and portable.

Margaret Middleton

Margaret Middleton is an independent exhibit designer and developer. She is also an avid advocate for inclusive practice in museums. She advocates online via Twitter, @magmidd, and she has been featured on the Incluseum. In particular, she has developed a Family-Inclusive Language Chart for museums. Margaret's chart has sparked conversations and awareness among museum professionals concerning how they talk to museum visitors. Most important, her work has unmasked many of the biases previously hidden by our daily language, such as assumptions of museum visitor gender (Middleton 2017). She recently contributed to MASS Action's toolkit. In addition to her advocacy role, Margaret is an active agent of inclusive practices within museums. Her work, *Barbie Gets with the Program*, pairs "Barbie playsets featuring computers and the real electronics on which they were based. The exhibit is organized chronologically

Figure 9.3. Barbie Gets with the Program.

Dario Impini, "*Barbie Gets with the Program*, 2017." Flickr, accessed November 4, 2017, https ://www .flickr.com/photos/infiniboudoir/3 3 73 8499026/in/album-72157681317663415/.

and explores women in computing over the years" (Middleton 2017). Margaret's work is intentional to both advocate for and implement inclusion in museums (see figure 9.3).

Mike Murawski

Mike Murawski is director of Education and Public Programs, Portland Art Museum. Mike is both an advocate for inclusion and an agent of inclusive practices within museums. He advocates for inclusion online via Twitter, @muraski27, and through the website he founded, artmuseumteaching.com. Although his website is a "digital community and collaborative online forum for reflecting on issues of teaching, learning, and experimental practice in the field of art museum education," he often advocates for inclusion, equity, and social justice through his posts (Murawski 2017b). In one of his latest posts, "Changing the Things We Cannot Accept—Museum Edition," Murawski lists the statements in figure 9.4.

Mike Murawski's Manifesto "Changing the Things We Cannot Accept – Museum Edition"

1. I cannot accept that museums are neutral.

2. I cannot accept that museums are entirely object-centered and their primary purpose is to serve and preserve their collections.

3. I cannot accept that museums function as separate from their communities.

4. I cannot accept the thought that involving community members and their knowledge in a museum's core practices will lower the quality of content and decrease overall trust in a museum's authority.

5. I cannot accept that museums do not consistently and persistently recognize the indigenous peoples on whose ancestral lands our institutions now stand.

6. I cannot accept that issues such as immigration, refugees, police violence, transgender rights, water, and climate change are too political for museums.

7. I cannot accept that museums still use 'keeping their donor base happy' as an excuse to not be socially relevant and forward thinking.

8. I cannot accept that many museums are hesitant or afraid to proclaim that Black Lives Matter and black life matters, or work with activists in the Movement for Black Lives and other intersectional movements standing up for human rights.

9. I cannot accept that, for museums, being socially responsible is just a liberal trend.

10. I cannot accept that we, as museum professionals and as citizens, do not fully recognize and celebrate the work we do to be inclusive, relevant, and responsive to the issues affecting the lives of our communities, our neighborhoods, our audiences, and our staff & volunteers.

Figure 9.4.   Mike Murawski's Manifesto.
Created by Laura-Edythe Coleman, derived from Murawski 2017a.

Figure 9.5.   "Museum Are Not Neutral" T-Shirt.
Murawski 2017c.

As you can see from the tone of Murawski's writing, he is prepared to advocate for inclusion and be an agent of inclusive practice in museums. He has been featured on the Incluseum, and he recently created a fashion trend with the museum professional community with his T-shirt design, "Museums Are Not Neutral" (see figure 9.5) (Murawski 2017c). He has also recently worked on the construction of MASS Action's toolkit.

Chris Taylor

Chris Taylor is chief inclusion officer of the Minnesota Historical Society. To my knowledge, he is the first person in an American museum to hold a position specifically tasked with creating inclusion. In fact, he heads the Department of Inclusion and Community Engagement to "guide internal and external strategies across all historic sites and museums to embed inclusive practices in our work to ensure the diversity of the state is reflected in all MNHS activities, including collections, programs, staffing, volunteers, historic preservation and governance" (Taylor 2015). In addition to his work as an agent of inclusive practices, Chris is an advocate for inclusion online via the Twitter handle @christaylordice. He speaks at museum conferences and has been featured on the Incluseum. He recently served as project advisor to MASS Action.

Architects of Inclusion

We have an increasing number of advocates, individuals articulating the importance of inclusion, and we have agents of change, those museum professionals who are putting words into action on a daily basis with their museums. We have only a few architects of inclusion: those individuals who see the larger picture of the museum field, understand the role of museums in society, and have a clear vision for how to advance inclusion in our institutions. The people who fit into this category are uniquely talented and perfectly poised to make substantial change within the museum field.

Elisabeth Callihan

Elisabeth Callihan is the head of Multi-Generational Learning at the Minneapolis Institute of Art. She advocates for inclusion online via Twitter, @bttyanne, and in person at museum conferences. She recently presented at the 2017 MuseumNext conference in Portland, explaining MASS Action, a project that she co-founded after reading an entry on the Incluseum blog (Callihan et al. 2017; Paquet Kinsley, Wittman, and Moore). Elisabeth proposed the Museum as Site for Social Action, or MASS Action, project to her employer, the Minneapolis Institute of Art in 2015. This three-year project has evolved, and recently Elisabeth stated, "MASS Action is not a project anymore. It is a network of people, individuals committed to seeing the museum field change, connecting in solidarity, recognizing there is strength in numbers. . . . That with enough voices, we can make change" (Callihan et al. 2017). Elisabeth is an advocate for inclusion and an agent of inclusionary practices within her museum. She is also an architect of inclusion through her work with MASS Action. It is no small feat to cast a vision to the museum profession and also arrange for "50 museum practitioners, representing museums of all sizes and types (art, history and historical sites, science, children's)" and to attend annual meetings in Minneapolis. At these annual conferences, the participants conversed "around topics of equity inside the museum, decolonizing practices, and authentic community-building" (Callihan et al. 2017). The MASS Action consortium has recently published a toolkit for practitioners and museums—a blueprint for social change.

Monica Montgomery

Monica Montgomery is the founder of the Museum of Impact and a self-proclaimed museum anarchist. She advocates for inclusion online via Twitter, @museumofimpact. Monica recently served as project advisor for MASS Action. Moved by the "grim reality of extralegal killings of black Americans and the #Black Lives Matter," she began tweeting. Her tweets led to the development of the Museum of Impact, the "first mobile social justice museum, inspiring action at the intersection of art, activism, self, and society" (Montgomery). As a mobile platform, Museum of Impact has the unique capability to move throughout the United States and address social issues as needed:

> Museum of Impact travels the country creatively activating spaces, fusing conscious content, art, and history to inspire action and build power. As a grassroots, progressive museum, we create pop-up experiential voyages into the heart of social movements; encouraging visitors to participate and leave their own mark, as they transform from bystanders to Upstanders. (Montgomery)

Monica is an advocate for inclusion, an agent of inclusionary practices, and an architect of inclusion. Her work with the Museum of Impact has generated a working model of inclusive practice from which museum practitioners and museums may learn.

Nina Simon

Nina has been making waves within the museum community for more than a decade. She is well known for her publications, *The Participatory Museum* and *The Art of Relevance*. She has been a steadfast advocate for inclusion, leveraging social media, blogs, and websites to communicate to a broad audience her thoughts on the social role of museums. She also speaks frequently at museum conferences concerning inclusion. In her 2015 MuseumNext talk, "Fighting for Inclusion," Nina outlined her call for museums to become more inclusive: "Here's my beef with inclusion: it's too good. No one is 'against' inclusion . . . but museums do exclude people. All the time" (Simon 2015). She spoke clearly to the fact that "inclusion isn't a given. Inclusion is something we fight for" (Simon 2015). Simon does fight for inclusion through her work at the Santa Cruz Museum of Art & History:

> But we didn't get there without a fight. We fought against common preconceptions of what a museum audience looks

like or who a museum is for. We fought against critics who claimed that we were dumbing down the museum. We fought overt and covert discrimination on the basis of age, race, and income. We fought our own biases, fears, and uncertainty . . . and we continue to do so today.

Nina is transparent and direct: inclusion is work—hard work. Yet she offers a blueprint for accomplishing inclusion: "We did it in two ways: by empowering individuals as participants in content creation, program design, and deep exploration of art and history; by connecting people across differences, building strong social bridges across race, age, economic background, and culture so that the transformed museum would be a place for everyone instead of a place for a particular target group. . . . These two changes are at the heart of inclusion." Her thought-provoking projects have engaged both museums and surrounding communities for years. The Santa Cruz Museum of Art & History reached its goals by adhering to four main concepts laid out in table 9.1.

I argue that Nina Simon is more than an advocate for inclusion and an agent for inclusive practices: she is an architect of inclusion. As an architect for inclusion, she casts a vision for what an inclusive museum should be and offers step-by-step solutions for building that museum. I see architects as individuals who propel movements with words, actions, and a vision of the greater plan. Nina Simon meets all three criteria for an architect of inclusion, and ultimately social change.

Table 9.1. Fight for Inclusion (Nina Simon)

1. Start Small	If you are fighting for inclusion, I ask you: *What small invitation could you make to be more inclusive?*
2. Arm Yourself	Going into battle? You're going to need a weapon. I want to briefly address three ways to arm yourself in the fight for inclusion (or whatever else you care most about): with strategy, with self-care, and with compatriots.
3. Make Space	*Where could you have more impact by making space for others?*
4. Start Within	*What's your fight?*

Adapted from Simon 2015 by Laura-Edythe Coleman.

Commit to Inclusion

In this chapter, we have seen a wide range of individuals, from an assortment of backgrounds. Each of these people are committed to promoting inclusion for museums. Many of those mentioned focus their activities on advocacy—speaking out about inclusion, equity, and social responsibility. Several of the individuals highlighted in this chapter have found specific ways to implement inclusive practice within their museums. And three individuals—Callihan, Montgomery, and Simon—represent a category that I call architects of inclusion. Each of these leaders casts a vision for the museum profession and blueprint to achieve that change. Where do you fit in? Are you an advocate? Are you an agent of inclusion? What would you like to be? In the next chapter, I will challenge you to take your place within the museum field.

10

Challenge to the Field

Become the Museum for Everyone

Museums are no longer about something, or even about someone. Museums are now about everyone. We must include everyone in our institutions from collections and preservation to exhibition design and programming. American museums have an opportunity relevant to society, to impact individuals and communities for the better. Are we willing to become the museum for everyone? What is the cost of becoming this new museum? Or, more important, what is the cost of not becoming the museum for everyone? Museums are, as ICOM states, in "service to society" (International Council of Museums 2007). In other words, museums are in service to humanity—not one human in particular, or even a group of humans, but humanity as a collective. Does our work reflect the ICOM definition of a museum? Why or why not? And what will it take to move us to change?

Government Policy

As a public institution, do we need guidelines for becoming an inclusive museum? For example, few museums were accessible before the Americans with Disabilities Act (ADA) (US Government 2015, 55). Our museums needed that push from the government to become accessible to all Americans. Are we as museum professionals proud of this example? Are we pleased that we needed to be told to become accessible? Or are we saddened or angered? If we truly believe museums should be accessible to all museum visitors, why did it take an act of law to prescribe the necessary changes for accessibility? We want to be relevant to society. Would government policy outlining our societal significance and enforcing inclusivity help to cement our social role? Do we honestly believe that such guidance would lessen our role in society? I do not know whether government policy is the answer to enforcing inclusion, but we, as a profession, should discuss all reasonable possible policies. Other nations have imposed inclusion within museums, with mixed results. In the United Kingdom, the government mandates, counts, and rewards institutions based on measurements of inclusion, and museums that receive UK funds must meet specific criteria for inclusivity. Museum professionals within the United Kingdom have criticized the government policies of inclusion. These critics dislike the enforced "quotas" through which museums must demonstrate that they have been inclusive of a certain number of "marginalized" people (Tlili 2008, 123–47). Museums must track these numbers and keep records. Do these mandated measurements help the UK museums to be more inclusive? Or are they merely, as some would claim, exercises in bean counting? At the very least, these mandates draw attention to the need for inclusion within their museums. Could the basic knowledge of the museum's surrounding community (gleaned by routine measurements) ensure that museum professionals are more aware of their community? Perhaps, but the argument remains that awareness does not necessarily equal engagement with the community.

American Alliance of Museums Accreditation and Inclusion

If government mandates are not possible or are too time consuming to create, what can we do now as a profession to ensure that American museums implement inclusion? The American

Alliance of Museums accredits those institutions that apply to become AAM museums and meet its criteria. American museums do not need accreditation from their profession to be in operation. An American museum does not necessarily have to align with AAM; the choice belongs to the institution. This is not to say that AAM accredits every museum that applies; there are strict guidelines that must be met to become an AAM museum (American Alliance of Museums "Eligibility Criteria"). Yet, unlike other fields in service to society, such as schools and daycares, or businesses such as restaurants and hotels, there is no organization that regulates museums as establishments. The American government does not regulate museums, nor are museums required to participate in professional self-regulation as guided by AAM. What if a museum decides to apply to AAM's accreditation program? Will that museum be required to demonstrate inclusivity? No. The American Alliance of Museums does not require proof of inclusive practice within member museums. How can this be? Is all the talk about museums' "Diversity, Equity, Inclusion and Accessibility" (DEIA) just talk? Are we as a profession proud to be aligned with those institutions that are exclusionary? I should think not. Could professional organizations, such as the American Alliance of Museums, require inclusive practice implementation within member organizations? I suggest that American museum professionals petition the American Alliance of Museums to require proof of inclusive practices within its member institutions. Again, will such a mandate change the level of inclusivity within American museums? Or will mandates on inclusion merely generate more bean counting work to be done? Perhaps an AAM requirement will provide greater awareness within museums about their inclusive and exclusive practices and about their role in society. What would happen if American museum professionals were required to learn about the communities in which their museums are located? What sort of change might happen? I propose that we, as museum professionals and members of AAM, require our member institutions to work toward inclusivity. Do we want to wait until the government requires that we become inclusive institutions?

Professional Education for Inclusion

How can we equip museum professionals to be more inclusive? Are we asking ourselves to do something that we have not been trained to do? Without adequate training and education, museum professionals attempting to implement inclusion may be setting themselves up for failure. How can we as a field allow our colleagues to attempt inclusion when they do not understand it? How can we learn more? Yes, there are books such as this one, and there are blogs and conferences. But is there formal training on how to make our museums more inclusive institutions? Not really. And yes, there should be a formal way to learn about inclusion. The American landscape has many undergraduate and graduate programs that could expand to cover the area of inclusion—if prompted. We have several prestigious museum studies programs such as Johns Hopkins University and George Washington University. But do we have specific museum programs for implementing inclusion on a professional level? No. We need to encourage higher education to create and deliver programs on inclusion for museum professionals. We should expect graduates from museum studies programs to have taken at least one course in inclusion (theory, history, implementation, and evaluation). We have the UK example of the University of Leicester's graduate program in the socially engaged museum practice—we could easily adapt such a program to fit the needs of American communities. What is stopping us from demanding adequate education for our museum professionals, especially for our future museum professionals? At the very least, we should expect regular continuing education courses that cover the implementation and evaluation of inclusion for museums. Current museum professionals may not have the ability to return to school for another graduate degree, and we should honor their service with adequate continuing education and certification programs for inclusion. These programs could be a joint effort of the AAM and universities. What would you like to know about inclusion? If our museum community needs professional education, we should fit our museum studies programs to meet that need.

The Cost

I know that, ultimately, almost every museum decision boils down to cost. Can we afford to change the way in which we do things? Is becoming an inclusive institution an expensive proposition? First of all, I would like to suggest that becoming an inclusive institution will be far less expensive than becoming an accessible one. For many museums, especially ones hosted by historical sites, adapting to accessibility guidelines was indeed expensive—architects, builders, and preservationists were required to alter older buildings. Evolving into an inclusive institution is not as expensive as the transformation required to become accessible. The cost will involve your museum relinquishing several prized possessions: institutional identity, curatorial authority, and time. First, is your museum ready to change what it is? Can you, as John Cotton Dana proposed in 1917, "fit your museum to meet those needs" (Dana 1917)? Are you willing to become what your community needs, as opposed to what you would like to remain to be? Why has it taken us one hundred years to reframe the words of John Cotton Dana as a question? You will need to let go of *who you are as an institution* to become the *institution that your community needs*. Second, you will need to relinquish curatorial authority. This may prove a painful process for you as an expert in your field, but, quite frankly, if no one cares to go to your museum, no one will ever know that you are an expert in your field. You may be able to tell many things about an object in your collection (provenance, preservation history, etc.), but you may not be able to put it in the personal context that an individual within your community can. Realize that most objects made by humans were for humans—quite literally to consume or to interact with. You may not be able to undo the museumification of an object within your collection, but you can allow others to shed their form of curatorial light upon it. And finally, there is time. Do you have the time to become an inclusive institution? Again I would ask, do you have the time not to be what your community needs? You have been an exclusive institution for long enough; try something new. It will cost you and your colleagues time—valuable time that could be spent on preservation or grant writing. I encourage you to take a leap of faith and sacrifice that time to build relationships with your community. The museums featured in this book that have successfully engaged inclusive practices, such as the Wing Luke Museum, have been able to obtain funding, gain volunteers, and bond with their communities. Why don't you have time to become what your community needs you to be?

Inclusion Is Here to Stay

Throughout this book, we have examined the theoretical background, history, and successful implementation of inclusion for museums. All of this writing is in vain if we do not attempt to change, to grow. To become an inclusive museum, you will need to know why we need inclusion—I discussed this topic in chapter 1. I encourage you to study chapter 2, covering the definition of *inclusion* and the historical relationship to the term *exclusion*. Learn about the spectrum of inclusion for museums, and ponder where on this spectrum your museum sits. Where do you want to be on the spectrum? Consider the advantages and disadvantages of inclusive practices, as outlined in chapter 3, and discuss these points with your colleagues. Embark on the journey to make your museum more inclusive through partnerships with people, as outlined in chapter 4. Create partnerships by being a museum that is personal, participatory, and portable. Grow relationships with like-minded social organizations, programs, and agencies in your community. Follow the transformational processes for these programs, as outlined in chapter 5. Look at the examples within this book—the Wing Luke Museum, the National Center for Civil and Human Rights, the New-York Historical Society. Decide to become a vehicle for broad social change, as described in chapter 6, and take a public stand as an institution that your museum is for everyone. Do not hide behind policies that you will never employ, such as the traditional "Diversity and Inclusion" policy addendum. Arm yourself with the tools to implement inclusive practice within your museum, and create your tools (if needed). Seek out those individuals who can partner with your museum as consultants for inclusion, as mentioned in chapter 7. Make sure to design a proper evaluation of inclusivity at the beginning of your journey. Leverage the quantitative and qualitative evaluation tools described in chapter 8 to create meaningful measurements of your institution's accomplishments toward becoming inclusive. Lastly, when you are unsure that you will succeed, when you want to give up, look to the individuals listed in chapter 9: advocates, agents, and architects of inclusion. These people are making a change, and you can too.

Ultimately, inclusion is an individual choice. Especially true in American society, in our democracy, in which we can choose who we are and what we do. No one person or even a society at large can truly mandate inclusion; we must choose to do so individually (Coleman et al. 2016).

Ask yourself these questions as an individual, and then take the answers back to your institutions: "How can I become less exclusive in my actions?" "What can I change today to be more inclusive?" "How can I advocate for change?" "When do I start becoming an agent and an architect of inclusion?"

Arm yourself with the knowledge and the tools, set a goal, and design a strategy. Spread the word and create interest. Conceptualize, and then construct your methods to implement and execute your plans. Build your foundation inside your museum, then outward into the community, inviting them back in to facilitate the co-creation of a place that includes them as an integral part of this new social norm.

Be a part of creating the next generation of inclusive museums by redeveloping the scope that defines our profession. Get out in front of it by building on the momentum of the inclusive movement that began in Europe, and help drive it forward into American museums. Advocate for new policies and procedures. Author professional courses, new programs, and evaluation techniques. Develop an alliance in your community, build an inclusive platform, and create a museum with everyone, by everyone, and for everyone.

Appendix

The Wing Luke Museum Community-Based Exhibition Model

WHAT WE VALUE

Our values direct what we do and how we do it. They impact every decision and interaction, sometimes in very subtle ways. Our values give us inspiration to keep going, through even the most challenging periods.

People give us meaning and purpose. Our institution is about people – the people whose stories are reflected in our walls, the people who work and volunteer throughout the year, the people who come to visit and experience, the people who came before us and the people who have yet to come. We are motivated by the elder sitting down to share a story long kept tucked away; the young adult sparked by seeing her likeness in a public space for the first time; the wide-eyed child soaking in the beats of lions dancing. We desire to be a place where people learn about themselves and others, grow in identity and awareness, connect with community, and take action to better society.

Relationships are our foundation. Through our work, we desire to connect people with people. We hope to build community within and across groups. We want people from different generations to learn from one another and grow together. We try to span economic and social class differences to reveal common backgrounds, integrated capabilities, and shared dreams. We desire to create opportunities for people to come together and build something new. We believe that together we are greater than the sum of our parts. We strive to build long-term relationships of respect and trust. Any exhibition project is not just a one-time opportunity but the beginning or continuation of a relationship with the understanding of commitment to future opportunities.

We desire community empowerment and ownership. Museums as purveyors of public knowledge and interpretation are powerful institutions. Who gets presented? How are they presented and under what terms? We strive to have community members – lay people who live history, preserve, transmit and create culture, and foster the arts – become empowered as they participate in our museum. We want to create ways for them to determine the course of projects, take action to see them carried out, and ultimately to own the stories and the projects, along with the Museum itself.

To do this, we have found the following:

The work is labor intensive. It takes time and effort to get to know people and build relationships. Communication becomes more demanding. We gather and maintain contact information, manage emails and phone calls, meet informally over coffee and lunch, hold evening and weekend meetings, and process pages and pages of meeting minutes. Decision-making becomes more complex as well. It takes time to attune to group dynamics and decision-making processes. Does voting by majority rules work? How about consensus through dialogue? What about deference to elders? We gather viewpoints, weigh opinions, and reach common understandings, all the while trying to make sure that each voice is heard.

The work requires flexibility. There are many more voices and personalities to take into consideration. We work according to the schedules of individuals with other jobs. We work with individuals who are exhibition-making for the first-time. New ideas and unforeseen circumstances can arise at any moment. We must be able to adjust, move and learn as we go along.

We willingly relinquish control. Museum staff does not seek individual, staff-directed vision. Our goal is to serve communities, seek out and learn their visions, and work to bring them to being. We cannot hold onto our own vision of the final product. That is not the point of the whole venture. Instead, we are about empowering others. Always listening and always being in the service of others can sometimes be taxing on our staff. Because community members lie at the heart of our work, criticism from them can hurt all the more.

"OUR INSTITUTION IS ABOUT PEOPLE – THE PEOPLE WHOSE STORIES ARE REFLECTED IN OUR WALLS, THE PEOPLE WHO WORK AND VOLUNTEER THROUGHOUT THE YEAR, THE PEOPLE WHO COME TO VISIT AND EXPERIENCE, THE PEOPLE WHO CAME BEFORE US AND THE PEOPLE WHO HAVE YET TO COME."

COMMUNITY-BASED EXHIBITION MODEL

"OUR GOAL IS TO SERVE COMMUNITIES, SEEK OUT AND
LEARN THEIR VISIONS, AND WORK TO BRING THEM TO BEING."

Our community-based exhibition model aims to integrate community
members throughout the process, from exhibition development to design
to fabrication and installation, and including exhibition fundraising,
publicity and marketing, education and public programming. We aim to
put community members in decision-making positions where they are
empowered to determine project direction, set priorities, make selections,
and guide project execution.

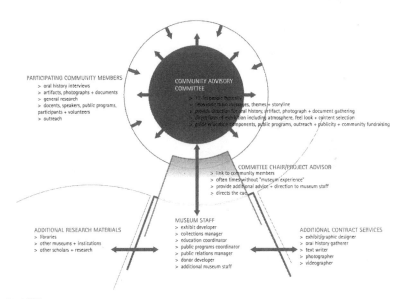

PARTICIPATING COMMUNITY MEMBERS
> oral history interviews
> artifacts, photographs + documents
> general research
> docents, speakers, public programs,
participants + volunteers
> outreach

COMMUNITY ADVISORY
COMMITTEE
> 15-30 people typically
> determine main messages, themes + storyline
> provide direction for oral history, artifact, photograph + document gathering
> direct look of exhibition including atmosphere, feel look + content selection
> guide education components, public programs, outreach + publicity + community fundraising

COMMITTEE CHAIR/PROJECT ADVISOR
> link to community members
> often times without "museum experience"
> provide additional advice + direction to museum staff
> directs the cac

ADDITIONAL RESEARCH MATERIALS
> libraries
> other museums + institutions
> other scholars + research

MUSEUM STAFF
> exhibit developer
> collections manager
> education coordinator
> public programs coordinator
> public relations manager
> donor developer
> additional museum staff

ADDITIONAL CONTRACT SERVICES
> exhibit/graphic designer
> oral history gatherer
> text writer
> photographer
> videographer

Diagram 1: Exhibit Team

140 / Appendix

EXHIBIT TEAM

On its most basic level, the Exhibit Team consists of:

- Museum staff
- Core community members
- Participating community members

Museum staff is charged with developing a community vision for an exhibition and bringing it into being. Since Museum staff has experience creating exhibitions, they serve as "technical advisors" for the community, providing input on exhibition components, feasibility and constructability, "project administrators", monitoring timelines and budgets, finding resources and facilitating communication, and "community organizers", mobilizing volunteers and bringing community members together toward a shared vision. Museum staff also uses professional contacts to gather research and materials from other institutions, where lay individuals may not normally have access.

Core community members include a Community Advisory Committee (CAC), typically ten to 15 individuals. CAC members have some direct connection with the exhibition topic, and they can be but are not necessarily leaders within other community organizations. They serve as the primary decision-making body within the Exhibit Team, and are charged with developing the main messages, themes, content and form of the exhibition and its related components. The CAC also serves to connect the project with other community members by inviting others to join the CAC, sharing about the project with family members, peers and community contacts, suggesting individuals for oral histories and artifact, photograph and document loans, and helping gather materials. For some projects, a Committee Chair or Project Advisor leads the CAC. This person takes a lead not because of any prior museum experience but because of his or her role within the community. The person directs the CAC, facilitating meetings, providing additional advice and direction to Museum staff, helping staff further connect with community members, and sharing their understanding of community dynamics.

Participating community members contribute to exhibitions in the following ways:

- Participating in and helping conduct oral history interviews, translating and transcribing
- Artifact, photograph and document loans and gathering
- General researchers in libraries, historical societies, museums and other institutions
- Outreach
- Serving as docents, speakers, public program participants and volunteers

EXHIBIT PROCESS

Our community-based exhibition model builds upon a basic exhibition development model but strives to infuse community members throughout the entire process. It can be broken down into seven stages.

Initial Outreach
Museum staff conducts Initial Outreach during the first stage of the process. Here we begin learning about the community and its dynamics, including existing leaders and organizations and their interrelationships, geographic concentrations, current issues and concerns, existing projects and initiatives, and marginalized groups within the community if existing along with other diversities. Museum staff share about the project, its origins, general timeline and initial goals, as well as about the Museum itself. We make phone calls, send emails and have face-to-face meetings. Often we print a simple

OUTREACHING TO POTENTIAL CAC MEMBERS
Outreaching to community members is a mix of visiting with established friends and initiating new relationships. Here are some outreach strategies:

Initiate relationships through small programs first and then build on these ongoing relationships.

Find out the current issues and events community members are passionate about and bring your resources and programming in line with those.

Diversify your Staff and Board and draw on their community understanding and connections.

Familiarize yourself with community organizations and organizers and then contact them to seek their advice on future projects, your current project idea and potential CAC members.

Ask people to recommend and invite others.

Dig for contact information, make cold contacts, visit individuals at their locations, invite them to your site, follow-up with emails and see what happens. Be open to the possibilities.

SELECTING CAC MEMBERS
While we are strategic about selecting CAC members, we also make room for flexibility. We consider the following as we form our CACs:

Include a mix of individuals who have participated on previous CACs and those who are new to exhibition-making.

Strategize the composition of the CAC. Some areas to consider within the mix include:

- Existing community leaders and authority figures
- Individuals able to bridge different groups within a single community
- Individuals able to think from different perspectives
- Individuals from diverse generations

Consider group dynamics and personalities. Will one person dominate the group? Will there be balanced discussion? Are there idea-generators and creative minds? What about "doers" within the group?

Include not only professional scholars and artists, but also everyday folk with lived experiences. Maintain an environment with everyone learning from one another. Watch for the tendency for individuals to defer to the recognized "experts" within the group. Sometimes deference also is given to "elders" so we also try to find ways for youth to feel comfortable sharing too. In the end, we have found that scholars and artists find it refreshing to hear first-hand testimonies and the everyday folk appreciate the opportunity to learn larger contexts, and the elders find it encouraging and affirming to hear from the youth and the youth are appreciative and honored to hear stories from the elders.

Seek commitments but don't require individuals to sign a commitment letter or participation contract. We hope that individuals will come to all of the meetings but understand that they are volunteers and trust that they will do their best.

Be open, welcoming, inviting and transparent. We encourage existing CAC members to invite others to come to the meetings. We know that it can be challenging to accommodate newcomers to the process but have chosen this route to remain open and welcoming and to place authority within the CAC itself.

MEETING 1	MEETING 2	MEETING 3
> *welcome and introductions* > *share project background, general timeline and cac role* > *identify audience* > *brainstorm main messages and themes*	> *revisit main messages and themes* > *prioritize main messages and themes*	> *confirm prioritized main messages* > *revisit prioritized themes* > *begin storyline development*

➡   ➡   ➡

MEETING 4	MEETING 5	MEETING 6
> *creation of storyline through bubble diagrams* > *brainstorm exhibition components*	> *review storyline* > *brainstorm look, feel, atmosphere of exhibition*	> *refine look, feel, atmosphere of exhibition*

➡   ➡

Diagram 2: CAC Meetings

brochure that includes a brief project description with goals and timeline, and a list of community partners if already established. Sometimes contact is made cold; we have just opened up the phone book and given a call or done a web search and sent an email. Usually a contact will result in referrals to others who might be appropriate, willing and interested.

While informal outreach is occurring, we start developing a list of potential CAC members. If we have worked with the community on a previous project, we have a head start and can already start to identify individuals. Often times we draw on the knowledge and connections of our Staff and Board.

At the end of Initial Outreach, we have a confirmed list of CAC members and are ready to hold our first meeting and begin Exhibit Development.

Key documents: Contact List, Project Outreach Brochure, CAC List

Exhibit Development
Exhibit Development occurs over several months of intensive meetings. The number, length, timing and location of the meetings depend on the dynamics of the community and the CAC. By the end of Exhibit Development, we have all the materials we need to move forward with Exhibit Design, assured that we have identified the vision, including the main messages, themes, content and form of the exhibition and its related components, desired by the CAC.

Below is an outline of Exhibit Development CAC meetings. The Meeting Facilitator has been the Museum Exhibit Developer or the Committee Chair/Project Advisor or the two working in tandem. At times we carry over brainstorming from one meeting to the next to provide CAC members more time to think about the ideas.

MEETING 1
Welcome and introductions – Facilitator welcomes and thanks CAC who then introduce themselves.

Share project background, general timeline and CAC role – Facilitator shares about the Museum, project background and timeline, and roles of Project Team members, especially the CAC. To help CAC members feel most comfortable, Museum Staff has found it helpful to review basic project information and roles to establish expectations before moving forward with

sharing content ideas. We also share with CAC members that in the end, no one individual will see his or her single vision created but hopefully everyone will see part of their vision and themselves in the final whole.

Identify audience – Here the Facilitator and CAC identify general Museum audiences along with particular project audiences. At times the CAC also prioritizes audiences if appropriate.

Brainstorm main messages and themes – Discussion centers on two questions: What should visitors who come to the exhibition learn? What are major areas/subjects/themes within the Community?

MEETING 2
Revisit main messages and themes – Museum Staff groups and re-writes brainstormed ideas for the CAC to review and further develop. Facilitator asks clarifying questions to draw out ideas further and seeks out areas that may have been overlooked.

Prioritize main messages and themes – At this point, with such a large host of ideas, we have found it helpful to have the CAC identify more prominent main messages and themes. We ask CAC members to select a certain number of main messages and themes that hold greater weight (generally anywhere from four to eight depending on the number of identified areas and the number of CAC members). After CAC members have marked their choices, we can see as a group desired areas of weight for the exhibition.

MEETING 3
Confirm prioritized main messages – Based on the brainstorming and prioritization in the previous meetings, Museum Staff writes formal statements for each main message, which are then presented to the CAC for review and revision. Main messages are those "take-away" messages that we hope each exhibition visitor learns.

Revisit prioritized themes – Facilitator also presents prioritized themes to the CAC for review and revision. Themes are topics, subject areas and motifs that are present in the exhibition. Group review and revision of main messages and themes is important to establish common understanding before moving forward to give physical shape to the exhibition.

Begin storyline development – The CAC brainstorms ways that exhibition visitors could learn about and experience the main messages and themes. Usually ideas for exhibition components have emerged throughout the early brainstorming process. Museum Staff keeps a record of these ideas, and the CAC now formally focuses on this aspect of Exhibit Development.

MEETING 4

Creation of storyline through bubble diagrams – Here the CAC divides into smaller groups, which are each charged with developing a diagram for a potential exhibition that encompasses the identified main messages and themes. Each group imagines the flow and order of the exhibition, along with visitor experiences. Small groups share back with the overall CAC. Through discussion, Facilitator asks clarifying questions to deepen understanding and gauge the CAC's desired direction for the exhibition, which could be in one or a combination of directions.

Brainstorm exhibition components – The CAC continues brainstorming exhibition components.

MEETING 5

Review storyline – Based on discussion in Meeting 4, Museum Staff creates a formal storyline diagram for review and revision by the CAC. Usually this storyline diagram is an amalgam of small group suggestions, though there may be a few options for the CAC to consider.

Brainstorm look, feel, atmosphere of exhibition – Facilitator asks the CAC to generate words and phrases describing all aspects of each part of the exhibition. What are visitors seeing, hearing, smelling, touching? What emotions should be evoked in each section? Is there an overall feeling that should be expressed? Are there variations within the exhibition?

MEETING 6

Refine look, feel, atmosphere of exhibition – The CAC continues brainstorming the look, feel and atmosphere of the exhibition. Facilitator asks clarifying and deepening questions and may seek CAC priorities as needed.

With each meeting, Museum Staff creates agendas, takes minutes and prepares necessary materials for the next meeting to keep the process moving forward. In between meetings, Museum Staff processes information provided by the CAC, refining and grouping it for review at the next meeting.

The aim for Museum Staff is to listen intently, internalize the CAC vision, and move the project forward, bringing Exhibit Development decisions before the CAC.

During this phase, we also begin oral history gathering, with the CAC developing and reviewing interview questions and refinements made according to the emerging exhibition main messages, themes and storylines. We also begin research for artifacts, photographs, documents and other materials, either in our collection, other institutions or people's homes.

Throughout this phase, we also discuss fundraising (budgets, community organizations and/or individuals to approach), publicity, marketing and outreach (strategies and contacts within the Community including community newspapers and organizations, as well as broad mainstream publicity; eventually we also review the exhibit title, opening reception invitation design and poster design with the CAC), education components (targeted schools and classes, tour content, hands-on activities) and public programs (audiences, ideas, venues and scheduling).

Key documents: Storyline Diagram, Interpretive Plan

FACILITATING CAC MEETINGS

Here are some creative ways to get CAC members sharing ideas and prioritizing them, along with some other tips to foster a welcome, open environment.

Incorporate an opportunity for all CAC members to speak and share early in your meeting. Too many meetings happen where Museum Staff talk and talk and talk, becoming the giver of information and the voice of authority rather than the recipient of information and the listening learner.

Use writing by CAC members in your meetings to allow for those who are less verbal to also share:

- Hand out "sticky notes" for individuals to write ideas for exhibitions – one idea per "sticky note". They can then place them in categories, building the sections of the exhibition.
- If a meeting is running long, but you still have a critical question you need input on, quickly hand out paper and ask CAC members to take a few minutes to respond. This exercise does not facilitate group discussion but does provide input from everyone.
- If you run out of time and have to cut a discussion short or if one person or just a few people tend to dominate a discussion, close out the meeting by handing out a piece of paper to everyone and asking them to write down any ideas that they did not have a chance to share. Collect the paper and incorporate responses into the meeting minutes.

At times break the CAC into smaller discussion groups. We ask for a recorder to write down ideas and a reporter to share back with the larger group. We use this exercise if we would like more in-depth ideas from across the group. We keep the CAC in a single large group if it is important to have consensus across the group and need to develop the CAC's shared vision.

Write ideas on large pieces of paper for the entire CAC to see. Seeing an idea in writing validates the person sharing and helps visual thinkers respond to ideas. When we review main messages and themes, we print them in the agenda but also write them on large sheets of paper or on an overhead so revisions can be made together in the large group.

Some methods to prioritize ideas with the CAC include:

- "Raise your hand" voting
- Placing a sticker or starring prioritized ideas
- Using different colored stickers to register different viewpoints

Look for opportunities to draw connections between individuals. Point out shared perspectives and ask follow-up questions to bring CAC members into dialogue with one another.

Look for opportunities to deepen understanding. Repeat or restate CAC members' comments to seek clarification. Ask follow-up questions to draw a better picture, elicit deeper ideas and uncover nuances. If we know that we need to move discussion forward, we look for opportunities to transition from an individual's comment to the next discussion area. At times CAC members bring up ideas outside of the agenda. It takes sensitivity to know when to allow a tangent to develop. Sometimes these conversations are necessary and the most insightful; at times they are better deferred to keep the dialogue moving forward.

018   WING LUKE ASIAN MUSEUM >   COMMUNITY-BASED EXHIBITION MODEL

Research and Gathering

Research and Gathering for an exhibition begins almost immediately. Museum Staff, interns and volunteers scour libraries, historic societies, museums, community organization files, news articles and online databases. We send inquiries via email to other institutions. We research through our own library and collection. From Initial Outreach and through the CAC, a list of individuals to contact for oral history interviews soon develops. Museum Staff, interns, CAC members and other volunteers conduct oral history interviews, with Museum Staff training volunteers, providing equipment, tracking contacts, and processing interviews. As the exhibition storyline and components emerge, Research and Gathering becomes more focused. Sometimes projects emerge such as video pieces and computer installations to further include oral histories and other materials in the exhibition.

Key documents: Oral History List, Research Files

Exhibit Design

Armed with decisions and direction from the CAC, we begin Exhibit Design. The Exhibit Designer uses the storyline, exhibition components, and descriptions of the exhibition look, feel and atmosphere to guide development of the physical space. From here, more diagrams, initial floor plans and sketches emerge.

During this time, the Project Team also selects specific materials for the exhibition. For oral histories, Museum Staff and select CAC members review transcripts and make notations according to the exhibition main messages, themes and storyline for eventual editing and use in the exhibition in either text, audio, video or computerized format. For artifacts, photographs and documents, original and photocopied materials are brought out for review and selection by the CAC. In the past, we have held a "selection day", when CAC members drop-in throughout the day, review materials, talk to Museum Staff, and use paper slips to mark compelling materials. This process allows CAC members to spend as much time as they have to go through materials. Museum Staff also can spend one-on-one time with CAC members to further understanding. The process also gives Museum Staff the opportunity to evaluate any "holes" in the exhibition and engage the CAC to conduct further gathering. Museum Staff then compiles CAC viewpoints and selections and prepares the Exhibit List for further review and refinement by the CAC.

With a refined Exhibit List, the Exhibit Designer proceeds with more specific plans and elevations. As time allows, the Exhibit Designer brings concepts and drawings to the CAC for input, review and feedback. CAC members provide valuable insight into general visitor experience as well as appropriateness of design and displays from an insider community perspective.

Key documents: Exhibit List, Design Layout, Design Elevations

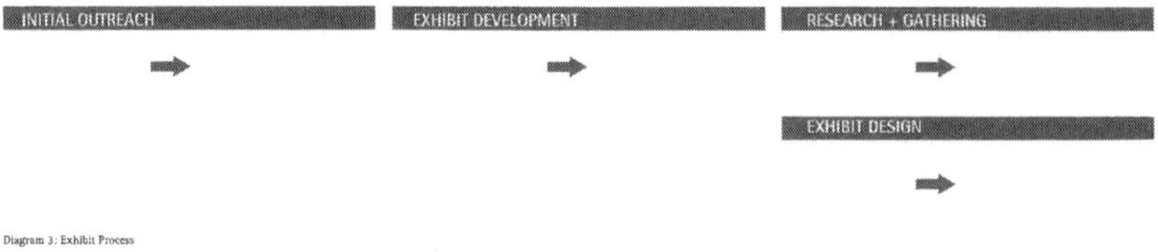

INITIAL OUTREACH   EXHIBIT DEVELOPMENT   RESEARCH + GATHERING

⇒   ⇒   ⇒

                                                              EXHIBIT DESIGN

                                                              ⇒

Diagram 3: Exhibit Process

Exhibit Fabrication and Installation

Exhibit Fabrication and Installation is completed most times through the efforts of Museum Staff, interns and a regular crew of volunteers, and at times through the use of contract workers. Typically we install over a 2½ week period. We invite CAC members to drop-in any time during installation. We hold a formal walk-through of the exhibition for CAC members prior to the opening. CAC members also help us install particular portions of the exhibition as needed.

Key documents: Exhibit Installation Schedule

Exhibit Opening

Our Exhibit Openings typically are held on Thursday evenings from 5:00 to 7:00 p.m. We send out invitations to Museum members and special invited guests, including the CAC, participating community members and other contacts. The program is short and includes thanks and acknowledgements from our Executive Director and brief sharing by select Community Participants as appropriate. We also coordinate beforehand with the CAC regarding food and other special touches for the Exhibit Opening.

Key documents: Exhibit Opening Program, Sign-in Sheet

Follow-up

Once an exhibition opens, some times additional community members come forth with stories and materials to share. They see examples of materials and stories, recognize similarities with their experience, and want to share too. We try to collect these additional oral histories and materials for our Collection.

We send thank you cards to the CAC and participating community members. At the end of the exhibition, we also send summary reports to community members, including attendance numbers and select exhibition comments. At times, we have sent evaluation surveys to CAC members and held evaluation meetings.

Key documents: Exhibit Summary Report

FACILITATING CAC MEETINGS (CONTINUED)

Incorporate CAC review throughout the process to remain accountable to the CAC and its vision. This includes review of key documents, exhibition materials and design, and a walk-through of the exhibition.

Honor people's time. Start CAC meetings near time (usually we provide a small grace window) and end on time even if you have not accomplished everything planned at the meeting. If we find we need to go over time, we ask for the group's permission to do so.

Treat the CAC as professionals. Send formal agendas ahead of time and meeting minutes promptly. We also send out two emails regarding upcoming meetings – one early for individuals to schedule and one close to the meeting as a reminder. Include a snapshot of the agenda in meeting notices so the CAC not only knows what to anticipate next but also sees purpose and productive value in meeting.

Provide food and drinks at the meetings. Food helps bring people together.

PARTNERSHIP EXAMPLES

Our Museum has partnered with a range of groups:

- Advocacy groups
- Arts collectives
- Business associations
- Community social organizations
- Cultural organizations
- Historic societies
- Housing developers
- Religious organizations
- Social service agencies
- Veterans organizations

Partnerships also have ranged in scale:

- Individuals
- 2-3 organizations with the Museum serving as the connector
- Multiple partnerships with 7-8 organizations working as a coalition
- Large extensive partnerships with organizations participating at different project levels

MODEL IN PRACTICE
SIKH COMMUNITY: OVER 100 YEARS IN THE PACIFIC NORTHWEST

In 2004, Museum Staff began work on an exhibition with the Sikh Community. We had been working with Sikh Community members increasingly since September 11, 2001, cultivating relationships with them and establishing our Museum as a place for them. Steps in this process included: invitation to participate in existing programs, revision of our permanent exhibition to include visible inclusion of the Community, and joint larger public programs. We also launched a long-term youth project with workshops on Sikhism and creation of an art installation and traveling exhibition, strategizing that working with youth first might be an easier way to extend relationships and build familiarity before working with adults on the onsite exhibition. Our Staff grew to include Sikh Community member Tripat Singh in a part-time position and our Board added Parminder Singh to its ranks as well.

In Summer 2004, we first met with Jasmit Singh, an active leader within The Sikh Coalition, to discuss the onsite exhibition. We had worked with Jasmit on the previous projects and had spoken with him along the way about the exhibition. It took a while to get momentum going on the project. We were still completing the youth traveling exhibition. Jasmit had a full plate, working full-time in the tech industry, raising a family, meeting the demands of his volunteer position at The Sikh Coalition, and remaining active in his Gurdwara, the Sikh focal place of worship and community. Even though we had worked with Jasmit over several years, we now turned attention to our exhibit process and shared with him about our community-based model. We met a few times during the summer to lay the foundation for the upcoming project.

In Fall 2004, we began asking about other community members to contact to form a CAC and start Exhibit Development. Initial Outreach lasted from September 2004 through February 2005. We created a general project brochure and an introductory email. Jasmit provided us with an initial contact list, and we set out to call and email individuals, sharing with them about the project and inviting them to participate in the CAC. We received recommendations to contact additional individuals. A community member also forwarded our email to others. Soon our list grew, individuals agreed to join the CAC, and it became time to set up the first meeting.

It was a challenge to find dates and times for CAC meetings. Knowing the busy schedules of community members, but also knowing that for the youth project, several community members were able to meet on Saturday mornings, we decided to hold our meetings on Saturday mornings too. We also decided to have fewer but longer meetings and to set the full schedule of meetings as best as we could anticipate right from the beginning.

We held our first CAC meeting on February 26, 2005. Our agenda began with welcome and introductions. Museum Staff for the exhibition consisted of: Exhibit Developer (project lead), Public Programs Coordinator (also the lead for the youth project), Director of Donor Development (fundraising contact), Public Relations Manager (publicity contact), Collections Manager (loans and permission to use, exhibit construction), and Exhibits Planner (exhibit design). We shared about the project background, answering questions such as "Why is the Museum doing this?" and "How does the exhibition fit into the bigger scheme of things?" Then we shared about our community-based exhibition process and the timeline for this particular exhibition. We transitioned to a basic summary of their role as the CAC including:

- Determine main messages of the exhibition
- Determine the major themes of the exhibition and its storyline
- Suggest names and provide contacts for interview subjects
- Identify artifacts and photographs as well as leads
- Advise on public programming, education activities, fundraising and publicity

During this first meeting, we brainstormed exhibition main messages and themes, asking the CAC to respond to the following questions: "What should visitors who come to the exhibition learn about the Sikh Community?" and "What are major areas/subjects/themes within the Sikh Community?" The CAC generated many ideas, some broad such as "historical aspects in the United States" and "contributions to the United States" and some more specific, naming specific waves of immigration, describing the experience of immigration not knowing the language or culture yet going with great courage, and pointing out key aspects of their faith including inclusivity, humility and protection. Later, as Museum Staff compiled meeting minutes, we grouped ideas into categories including: general approach, history, immigration, settlement, contributions, second/third generations, religion, culture, perceptions of the community, assimilation-integration, demographics and contemporary issues, other, and additional ideas (which included ideas about exhibition components). At the first meeting, CAC members also shared insightful approaches to the exhibition, indicating not just the "what" but also the "how". "We don't want to dilute or take away from the religion but we don't want to go 'overboard' to make [the exhibition] inaccessible to the general public." "Right now, [Sikhism] doesn't fit into people's minds. [We] want to share that 'we are a part of the world.'" Towards the end of the meeting, the CAC discussed oral history and material gathering, centered around the question, "Based on these areas, whom can we talk to?" and "What should we ask them?" The CAC also talked about public programming ideas, which was not in our initial agenda but which the group had great energy around. At the close of this meeting, we encouraged the CAC to send us names of individuals to join the CAC and individuals for oral history and material gathering.

Our second meeting was held on March 5, 2005. Prior to the meeting, Museum Staff, having listened to the discussion at the first meeting, drafted an overview statement and six main messages for review and refinement by the CAC. These main messages would be the "take-away" messages we hoped visitors would gain through the exhibition and would guide further Exhibit Development. Group review allowed us to refine the statements with greater specificity, confirm shared focal points, and check for large areas overlooked in the previous discussion. The overview statement and main messages for this exhibition were:

The Sikh Community has long roots in the Pacific Northwest, spanning from the late 1800s to the present day. We have made rich contributions to our region in diverse professions. Being Sikh is determined by our religious faith, now the 5th largest faith in the world. We have faced racism, discrimination, stereotypes and mis-identity, as well as issues of assimilation and acculturation, but have emerged as an established community in the United States.

1. The Sikh Community has long roots in the Pacific Northwest and the United States. From the day we landed in Vancouver and Bellingham, to our migration through Washington to California, and on to the rest of the nation, the Sikh Community has a presence in all parts of our country.

2. The primary waves of immigration for the Sikh Community in the United States are: 1880s-1890s early laborers comprised of mostly men; 1910s-1940s reverse migration for freedom fight in South Asia; 1960s professionals with families and an emerging community; 1980s response to political upheavals in India; 1990s professionals and the established community.

3. The Sikh Community has made rich contributions to the Pacific Northwest and our nation. Sikhs have distinguished themselves in diverse professions and in American life. First, second and third generations of Sikhs have been in professional life and continue to make contributions to our nation.

4. Being Sikh is determined by our religious faith, not our ethnic identity. The Sikh faith was founded in 1469 by Guru Nanak in Punjab, South Asia, and has spread throughout the globe, becoming the 5th largest faith in the world. Our personal identity and community life is rooted in our religious faith and for some, includes ties to South Asia and its culture.

5. The Sikh Community has been impacted by perceptions of the larger community throughout its history in the Pacific Northwest, including racism, discrimination, stereotypes and mis-identity. The tragic events of September 11, 2001 have had a particularly strong, recent impact on the Sikh Community.

6. Like other immigrant communities, the Sikh Community faces issues of assimilation and integration in the United States. With a now established community and significant demographic presence in certain areas in the Pacific Northwest, the Sikh Community faces additional issues in contemporary times as well as in the future.

We reviewed the statements and then continued our discussion of major areas, subjects and themes for the exhibition. Follow-up in the second meeting provided the CAC an opportunity to look with a fresh eye, providing more detail and filling in oversights. At the end of the discussion, each CAC member received four stickers to place next to four "priorities" for the exhibition. This process allowed us to register select "areas of weight", which would then help guide storyline development, the meeting's next agenda item. Here were the "weights" for this exhibition:

History (6)
Contributions (6)
Perceptions of the Community (6)
Assimilation-Integration (6)
Religion (5)
Demographics and Contemporary Issues (4)
Culture (3)
Second/Third Generations (2)
Settlement (1)
Other (1)

Since the group had less familiarity with previous Museum community-based exhibitions and preferred to have as much background and contextual information as possible to make decisions, Museum Staff decided to share example images from past exhibitions before moving forward with storyline development, a fun but challenging part of Exhibit Development. In storyline development, we order and weave together the various areas of the exhibition into a coherent whole. To do this, we broke into three small groups. Each group was given a large piece of paper and a set of colored pens to take a stab at diagramming the exhibition in light of the following questions: "How do the messages and themes fit together into a space?" "Are there sections?" and "In what order and/or relationships?" We shared at the start that typically there would be parts from each group's vision that come together to create a rich whole. Each group then worked to complete a storyline and presented it back to the CAC. Although we had hoped to talk more about oral history and material gathering, specific follow-up areas for individual CAC members, and fundraising at this meeting, time ran out and we had to defer this discussion to the next meeting, set for March 26, 2005.

Introduction. Sikh Community: Over 100 Years in the Pacific Northwest
(2005, Main Gallery)

At this meeting, we started off reviewing various follow-up areas, including fundraising, publicity and outreach, and public programming. This exercise became a regular part of future meetings so we could track plans, follow-up action items, and mark completed tasks. We then revisited storyline development. Again, in between the meetings, Museum Staff reviewed the storylines generated by the three small groups and tried to weave them together into a whole, incorporating ideas from the various groups all in the context of the established main messages and prioritized areas of weight. The CAC reviewed the storyline, and upon consensus, we then moved forward to discuss the look and feel of the overall exhibition and each section, addressing the questions: "What are visitors seeing, hearing, touching, smelling in each section of the exhibition?" "What are they feeling?" and "What emotions are associated with each section?" Discussion was very lively and impassioned. CAC members shared their own personal experiences, feelings and emotions being Sikh in the United States and expressed their viewpoints about the overall spirit of the exhibition. CAC members stated that they wanted the exhibition to be upbeat with high spirits, proclaiming that the Community had faced troubles but had pushed through. Bright colors would offset historic black and white photographs. Other CAC members mentioned that at times living in the U.S. can feel limiting; you are judged by people before they know who you are, and you can feel restricted and held back.

At one point in the meeting, there seemed to be a generational divide in viewpoints, where older CAC members held to an overall upbeat spirit throughout the exhibition while younger CAC members emphasized the weight and burdens carried by the Community. At the meeting, this difference was not explored, and instead, one perspective held sway over the other and one viewpoint felt more marginalized than the other. Upon reflection, Museum Staff recognized a missed opportunity for intergenerational learning right then and there. Recognizing what had happened, Museum Staff followed-up the meeting with personal discussions and if needed, apologies. We then tried to allow for both viewpoints in the exhibition.

Our next meeting was held on June 4, 2005. Here Museum Staff had planned to assess gathered materials with the CAC to be able to start firming up the Exhibit List. Most of this meeting however was spent reviewing our follow-up areas – all very necessary and important but not what we had planned. We reviewed poster options for a Call for Materials for early publicity and outreach. We discussed the exhibition title, which then went on to be a lengthy email discussion. We discussed fundraising initiatives. Towards the end of the meeting, we briefly reviewed materials but not nearly as in-depth as we needed.

Following this meeting, several observations arose. Museum Staff and the CAC recognized that with the exhibition set to open in the Fall, we needed to meet with greater frequency (rather than tailing off from CAC meetings, which might happen with other projects at this point), and we really needed to focus on identifying and gathering more exhibition materials. We held our next meeting on June 30, 2005. In the meantime, we had produced a poster and Call for Materials and distributed them to Gurdwaras and libraries along the West Coast of the United States and Canada. The CAC made plans to visit a Gurdwara in Bellingham in July to further outreach, and we identified a few individuals to serve as primary contacts for fundraising. Museum Staff had also contracted with a Graphic Designer, Videographer and Oral History Gatherer for the project. At the June 30th meeting, we reviewed the emerging list of exhibition materials, including a list of potential video pieces. The CAC named specific items to add, individuals agreed to gather them, and we set our next meeting for the end of July.

150 / Appendix

In between these two meetings, we made the momentous decision to move the start of the exhibition. Based on our experience to date, knowing the CAC decision-making process, and evaluating the remaining scope of work, we knew we needed more time. Since we had not yet sent out invitations or major publicity materials, we changed the opening date from September 23 to October 21. Prior to the July meeting, the CAC met at a member's home to review each video piece and make determinations for the exhibition. In the end, the CAC decided to create just one video piece ourselves – on-the-street interviews to provide the hook at the start of the exhibition. It became the Museum Staff's role to track down the other pieces, get permission to use them, and prepare them for presentation in the exhibition. At the July meeting, we went through the Exhibit List in detail, isolating additional photographs, objects and artwork, reviewing individuals for the Contributions section, and moving some community organizations from feature in the Contributions section to the Historic Timeline instead.

In the August 11th meeting, we continued to cull through exhibition materials. We also reviewed education activities for the exhibition. On August 31, we met again to discuss follow-up areas. We completed a mailing of 408 letters to community members with a flier on the exhibition, a donation form and return envelope. We talked about other fundraising initiatives. We went into further detail for public programming and started looking at calendars for scheduling.

September 17 and 24 marked two critical meetings. Museum Staff pulled out all of the gathered materials listed in our draft Exhibit List. Prior to these meetings, CAC members already had looked at photographs and documents and marked desired materials for the exhibition. Now at these two meetings, we reviewed the Exhibit Layout, each individual section, and each item for possible inclusion in the exhibition. Ultimately, the CAC reviewed the materials three times – once on the 17th and then again on the 24th with members who could not make the first review. On the 24th, later in the day, a key officer in the Renton Gurdwara also arrived to review the materials. By this time, instead of Museum Staff directing the review, members of the CAC themselves shared their work with the officer.

Our final formal CAC meeting occurred on September 28, 2005. We talked extensively about publicity and outreach and then made plans for the opening reception, including greeters, food and drinks, program speakers, print materials, dress code and the invitation mailing. Exhibit Installation began on October 3, with regular exhibition volunteers helping with construction and painting, and Museum Staff coordinating materials. A contract Writer wrote text introducing each main exhibition section. Museum Staff along with a CAC member wrote labels. All of the text was reviewed and finalized by Jasmit Singh of The Sikh Coalition. On October 18, 2005, just two days before the opening reception, the CAC held a walk-through of the exhibition. It was important for the CAC to view the exhibition prior to the opening so they could feel comfortable sharing the exhibition with others. At this time, CAC members also dressed mannequins and advised on case displays.

EVALUATION

We use both quantitative and qualitative measurements to evaluate our exhibitions:

- Audience numbers, including onsite exhibition (general visitors and school tours) and public programming
- Community participant numbers, including new and returning CAC members, oral history interviewees, interviewers and transcribers, artifact, photograph and document loaners, other contributors, and community fundraising donations
- News articles and web features including both mainstream and community press
- Surveys including visitor surveys, CAC surveys and public programming surveys
- Visitor comments in exhibition comment books

FUNDRAISING

We have received funding for this work from a range of sources, seeking government, private foundation and corporate (including foundation, community relations and marketing sources) support. In addition we have sought support from organizations and individuals in the communities themselves.

Here are levels of support we have used in the past to approach community organizations for some projects, as appropriate. We approach organizations not only for financial support but also endorsement and outreach. In return, organizations receive recognition in our newsletter, website, exhibition credit panel and publicity materials. As we ask other organizations for support, we also support their work along similar lines.

- Contributing Organization: The organization agrees to have a representative from their organization serve on the CAC OR make a contribution of $_____ to the project (minimum $350).

- Supporting Organization: The organization agrees to provide publicity in the organization's newsletter or other publicity materials, AND make a contribution of $_____ to the project (minimum $75).

- Endorsing Organization: The organization agrees to have a representative from their organization participate in a related event for the project, AND/OR provide publicity in the organization's newsletter or other publicity materials.

With some exhibition projects, we also send letters to individuals asking for donations to support the project. The letter is typically co-signed by our Museum Executive Director and a community leader involved in the project. Community partners also have contributed mailing lists, expanding the reach of the exhibition and our Museum. Sometimes CAC members also decide to send personal letters asking for support from their peers.

Opening day was an amazing, energy-filled day for Museum Staff and community members. A reporter from a major newspaper came to interview CAC members and take photographs. The national director of The Sikh Coalition also flew out to Seattle from New York to view the exhibition and celebrate the accomplishment. It was great affirmation of the community-based exhibition process to witness CAC members guiding family and friends through the exhibition and to see so many community members come to celebrate the opening.

The exhibition was up from October 21, 2005 through April 16, 2006. We had a total of 6,796 visitors, which is equivalent to our regular attendance for that time period. Our school tour attendance was 4,055. We held four public programs during the run of the exhibition, including the opening reception, film showing of *Continuous Journey*, an artist workshop with illustrator Vishavjit Singh of Sikhtoons.com, and the closing program *Images through the Ages*. What distinguished these programs from previous exhibition programming was the number of out-of-town participants coming to present, since the CAC desired to use limited resources to have programs with individuals who the local Sikh Community might not normally have the opportunity to see.

We conducted a visitor survey during the exhibition to fulfill a grant requirement, help us gain feedback on our work, and to be able to share information back to our community participants. We found that many respondents were first-time visitors, coming for the new temporary exhibition, having been recommended by friends or family members. Several survey comments indicated attendance to the exhibition by Sikh Community members. Four respondents identified themselves directly as Sikhs. A few indicated hearing about the exhibition through their Gurdwara. One visitor's anecdotal comment about being the only non-Sikh visitor there at the time also provided a glimpse into some of our exhibition audience. While we were not able to quantify Sikh attendance, we were excited that there were several indicators of exhibition attendance by Sikh Community members.

Beyond just attendance, we had desired that Sikh Community members would feel pride about their own personal stories, their community and faith and would be able to share their own stories and share about their community and faith. There were 22 Sikh Community advisors for the exhibition. Thirteen of them also shared their stories through oral history interviews. Eleven of them recommended other Sikh Community members for oral history interviews. We conducted 29 oral histories total; 14 individuals loaned personal photographs, artifacts and documents for the exhibition. Two Sikh Community members helped conduct oral history interviews for the project. The national director of The Sikh Coalition attended both the exhibition opening reception and the final public program through support of the Sikh Community itself. The Sikh Coalition also worked with filmmaker Kevin Lee to document its work in Seattle, including its partnerships and the exhibition.

CHALLENGES

We recognize several challenges associated with the community-based exhibition model:

The community-based exhibition model is very labor intensive and process-oriented. While we have had no easy answers to staff-burnout, we try to keep our eye on project goals, celebrate accomplishments, and maintain a sense of humor.

The model requires Museum Staff to organize many individuals. Communication is key. We start contact lists early and include a memo section to track communication.

Roles within the model are highly interdependent. We strive to maintain communication among Museum Staff too. Project electronic files are kept on a common server for Museum Staff to access. We update Museum Staff on Exhibit Development progress, invite them to CAC meetings, distribute CAC minutes to all Museum Staff, and have Interdepartmental Meetings focused on a specific exhibition project, along with regular updates in all Staff Meetings.

We train volunteers in specialized skills, such as oral history gathering. We value community participation on all levels, individual learning, personal growth and community connections.

The Museum becomes involved in community dynamics. We try to always offer a listening, learning ear and remain a place for many, not just a select few, to share. In this spirit, we make informal calls to CAC members and community participants throughout the project. The Museum can serve as a meeting ground for diverse viewpoints. We try to build ties with key community advocates who can cross over groups within a single community. We also understand and respect when a community is not ready to tell a particular story.

We attempt to serve many communities and many demands. Since communities know that we strive to create and maintain long-term relationships, they tend to be more patient, understanding and supportive.

CLOSING

The community-based exhibition model is ever-evolving. For more resources on the community-based exhibition model, visit our website at www.wingluke.org.

Resources

Chapter 6: Driving Broad Social Change: Becoming a Vehicle

UK Policies on Inclusion for Museums, Department of Culture, Media, and Sport: http://webarchive.nationalarchives.gov.uk/20100113222743/; http://www.cep.culture.gov.uk/images/publications/centers_social_change.pdf

The National Archives, Access for All Toolkit, enabling inclusion for museums, libraries, and archives: http://webarchive.national archives.gov.uk/20081208232134/; http://www.mla.gov.uk/policy/Inclusion/MLA_Activity_on_Social_Inclusion

Museums Association, Museum Manifesto for Tolerance and Inclusion: http://www.museumsassociation.org/download?id=1214164

Museums Association, Valuing Diversity—The Case for Inclusive Museums: http://www.museumsassociation.org/download?id=1194934

University of Leicester, Professor Richard Sandell, social inclusion, museums, and the dynamics of sectoral change: https://lra.le.ac.uk/bitstream/2381/52/1/mands4.pdf

University of Leicester, Museums and Social Inclusion, the GLLAM Report: https://www2.le.ac.uk/departments/museumstudies/rcmg/projects/museums-and-social-inclusion-the-gllam-report/GLLAM%20Interior.pdf

Chapter 7: Tools for Implementing Inclusion in Your Museum

Margaret Middleton's Family-Inclusive Language Chart: https://www
.margaretmiddleton.com/family-inclusion

Taboo Incluseum Edition Game: https://incluseum.files.wordpress
.com/2015/10/incluseumgame.pdf

LGTBQ Alliance Welcoming Guidelines for Museums: http://aam-us
.org/docs/default-source/professional-networks/lgbtq_welcome
_guide.pdf

National Informal Stem Education Network Museum & Community Partnerships, Collaboration Guide: http://www.nisenet.org/
collaboration-guide

Museum/Community Partnerships: Lessons Learned from the Bridges Conference: https://www.fi.edu/sites/default/files/Evaluation
Reasearch_2MuseumCommunityPartnerships2011.pdf

Community-Based Exhibition Model, printed book available from the Wing Luke Museum of the Asian Pacific American Experience: http://www.wingluke.org/community-process

Chapter 8: Tools for Evaluating Inclusion in Your Museum

Sources for Demographic Data in the United States

IMLS, Museum Universe Data: https://www.imls.gov/research
-tools/data-collection

Museum Mapping and Demographics: http://museumstat.org/

US Census Data: https://www.census.gov/data.html

Pew Research Center: http://www.pewresearch.org/download
-datasets/

Evaluation Tool Sources

IMLS: https://www.imls.gov/research-evaluation/evaluation
-resources

Visitor Studies Association: http://www.visitorstudies.org/

Texts for Survey Question Development

Bradburn, Norman M., Brian Wansink, and Seymour Sudman. 2004. *Asking Questions: The Definitive Guide to Questionnaire Design — for Market Research, Political Polls, and Social and Health Questionnaires.* San Francisco: Jossey-Bass.
Fowler, Floyd J., Jr. 2013. *Survey Research Methods.* Los Angeles: Sage.
Salant, Priscilla, and Don A. Dillman. 1994. *How to Conduct Your Own Survey: Leading Professionals Give You Proven Techniques for Getting Reliable Results.* New York: John Wiley & Sons.

Social Capital Integrated Questionnaire (SCIQ) Description

The authors of the SCIQ emphasize the need for adaption thusly: the instrument "tries to strike a balance between conceptual rigor and cross-cultural flexibility and adaptability . . . any application will require adaptation to the local setting" (Christiaan Grootaert, *Measuring Social Capital: An Integrated Questionnaire* [Washington, DC: World Bank, 2004], 6). It is a testament to the rigor of the instrument that it must be adapted. The SCIQ authors offer the following adaptation suggestions:

1. The researchers study the six modules of the SCIQ and decide an appropriate balance among the indicators addressed. It is anticipated that researchers will use only the modules needed to explore the social indicators of the local setting.
2. The researchers should study the individual questions and answer codes of the SCIQ to determine the relevance of each question/answer to the local context. Inappropriate questions/answers should be removed.
3. The researchers should examine the language of the SCIQ. It was originally written in English, and should translation be necessary, it should be carefully crafted to maintain the meaning, losing as few of the nuances as possible.
4. The researchers should adhere to standards concerning training of surveyors, pilot testing, and data collection.

SCIQ (Original) Excerpts

5. Social Cohesion and Inclusion

5.1. How strong is the feeling of togetherness or closeness in your village/neighborhood? Use a five-point scale where 1 means feeling very distant and 5 means feeling very close.
1 Very distant
2 Somewhat distant
3 Neither distant nor close
4 Somewhat close
5 Very close

5.2. There are often differences in characteristics between people living in the same village/neighborhood: for example, differences in wealth, income, social status, ethnic background, race, caste, or tribe. There can also be differences in religious or political beliefs, or there can be differences due to age or sex. To what extent do any such differences characterize your village/neighborhood?
Use a five-point scale where 1 means to a very great extent and 5 means to a very small extent.
1 To a very great extent
2 To a great extent
3 Neither great nor small extent
4 To a small extent
5 To a very small extent

5.3. Do any of these differences cause problems?
1 Yes
2 No → go to question 5.6

5.4. Which two differences most often cause problems?
1 Differences in education
2 Differences in landholding
3 Differences in wealth/material possessions
4 Differences in social status
5 Differences between men and women
6 Differences between younger and older generations
7 Differences between long-term and recent residents
8 Differences in political party affiliations
9 Differences in religious beliefs

10 Differences in ethnic background/race/caste/tribe
11 Other differences

5.5. Have these problems ever led to violence?
1 Yes
2 No

Conflict-Related Items and Exhibition

I am now going to ask about the collection at your cultural heritage institution.

5.24. Thinking about your collection, does your collection reflect the community in the surrounding neighborhood?
1 Yes
2 No → go to question 5.25

Use a five-point scale where 1 means to a very great extent and 5 means to a very small extent.
1 To a very great extent
2 To a great extent
3 Neither great nor small extent
4 To a small extent
5 To a very small extent

5.25. In your opinion, does the content of your cultural heritage institutions collection represent generally peaceful history, or is it marked by violence?
1 Very peaceful
2 Moderately peaceful
3 Neither peaceful nor violent
4 Moderately violent
5 Very violent

5.26. To what extent do government policies concerning social inclusion pertain to your work at your cultural heritage institution?
1 A lot
2 A little
3 Not at all

Ethical Conduct of Research

Citi Training for Researchers: https://www.citiprogram.org/rcrpage
.asp
Social Research Association: http://the-sra.org.uk/wp-content/
uploads/ethics03.pdf

Coding and Analysis of Data

Schutt, Russell K. 2012. *Investigating the Social World: The Process and Practice of Research*, 7th ed. Thousand Oaks, CA: Sage.
Talja, Sanna. 1999. "Analyzing Qualitative Interview Data: The Discourse Analytic Method." *Library & Information Science Research* 21 (4): 459–77.

Interviewing

Foddy, William H. 1993. *Constructing Questions for Interviews and Questionnaires: Theory and Practice in Social Research*. Cambridge: Cambridge University Press.
Miller, William, and Benjamin Crabtree. 2004. "Depth Interviewing." In *Approaches to Qualitative Research: A Reader on Theory and Practice*. Edited by Sharlene Nagy Hesse-Biber and Patricia Leavy. New York: Oxford University Press.
Seidman, Irving. 1998. *Interviewing as Qualitative Research: A Guide for Researchers in Education and the Social Sciences*, 2nd ed. New York: Teachers College Press.

Research Software

NVivo Qualitative Research Software: http://www.qsrinternational
.com/nvivo/what-is-nvivo
SPSS Quantitative Research Software: https://www.ibm.com/
products/spss-statistics

Bibliography

American Alliance of Museums. 2015. "2015 MUSE Awards." Accessed January 15, 2016. http://aam-us.org/about-us/grants-awards-and-competitions/muse-awards/past-award-winners/2015-muse-awards.

———. "About Us: Strategic Plan American Alliance of Museums." Accessed July 27, 2017. http://www.aam-us.org/about-us/strategic-plan.

———. "American Alliance of Museums' Strategic Plan." Accessed August 11, 2017. http://www.aam-us.org/about-us/strategic-plan.

———. "Diversity and Inclusion Policy." Accessed January 18, 2017. http://www.aam-us.org/about-us/who-we-are/strategic-plan/diversity-and-inclusion-policy.

———. "Eligibility Criteria." Accessed November 7, 2017. http://www.aam-us.org/resources/assessment-programs/accreditation/eligibility.

Atkinson, A. B., and United Nations. 2010. *Analysing and Measuring Social Inclusion in a Global Context.* New York: United Nations.

Babbie, Earl R. 2009. *The Practice of Social Research*, 12th ed. Australia: Wadsworth, Cengage Learning.

Bailey, Dina A. 2017. *Teachable Moments: Lessons to Take to Heart.* National Council on Public History. http://ncph.org/history-at-work/teachable-moments-lessons-to-take-to-heart/.

Berger, Peter L., and Thomas Luckmann. 1990. *The Social Construction of Reality: A Treatise in the Sociology of Knowledge.* New York: Anchor Books.

Bonilla, Yarimar, and Jonathan Rosa. 2015. "#Ferguson: Digital Protest, Hashtag Ethnography, and the Racial Politics of Social Media in the United States." *American Ethnologist* 42 (1): 4–17.

Bryant-Greenwell, Kayleigh. 2014. "Speaking & Writing." *Curatorally.* https://curatorally.com/writing/.

———. 2015. "Programs." *Curatorally.* https://curatorally.com/awards/.

———. 2017. "A Seat at the Table." *Curatorally.* https://curatorally.com/awards/a-seat-at-the-table/.

Bryman, Alan. 1984. "The Debate about Quantitative and Qualitative Research: A Question of Method or Epistemology?" *British Journal of Sociology* 35 (1): 75–92. http://www.jstor.org/stable/590553.

Buchanan, Larry. 2014. "What Happened in Ferguson?" *New York Times,* updated August 10, 2015. https://www.nytimes.com/interactive/2014/08/13/us/ferguson-missouri-town-under-siege-after-police-shooting.html.

Callihan, Elisabeth, et al. 2017. *MASS Action Toolkit.*

Cardiel, Chris, and Jennifer Borland. 2015. *Representing Diversity: Advocating for Inclusive Development and Evaluation.* Association of Science-Technology Centers.

CARE. "CARE and the National Center for Civil and Human Rights, Inc., Celebrate International Day of the Girl." Accessed October 28, 2017. https://www.care.org/newsroom/press/press-releases/care-and-national-center-civil-and-human-rights-inc-celebrate.

Center for the Future of Museums. 2010. *Museums & Society 2034: Trends and Potential Futures.* Center for the Future of Museums.

———. 2015. *Center for the Future of Museums: Unsafe Ideas: Building Museum Worker Solidarity for Social Justice.* Center for the Future of Museums.

Chasmer, Jessica. 2015. "Michelle Obama Says Black Kids Feel Unwelcome at Museums, Cultural Institutions." *Washington Times,* May 6. Accessed September 26, 2017. https://www.washingtontimes.com/news/2015/may/6/michelle-obama-says-black-kids-feel-unwelcome-in-m/.

Chinn, Cassie. "About Us > Wing Luke Museum." Accessed December 13, 2017. http://www.wingluke.org/about/.

———. 2006a. *Community-Based Exhibition Model.* Seattle, WA: Wing Luke Asian Museum.

———. 2006b. *The Wing Luke Asian Museum: Community-Based Exhibition Model.* Seattle, WA: Wing Luke Asian Museum.

———. 2016. "Community Process > Wing Luke Museum." Accessed December 16, 2015. http://www.wingluke.org/community-process.

Coleman, Laura-Edythe. 2015. "Social Inclusion and the Gatekeeping Mechanisms of Curatorial Voice: Are Museums Ready to Be Agents of Social Justice?" In *Progressive Community Action: Critical Theory and Social Justice in Library and Information Science*. Edited by Bharat Mehra and Kevin Rioux. Sacramento: Library Juice Press.

———. 2016a. "The Socially Inclusive Museum: A Typology Re-Imagined." *International Journal of the Inclusive Museum* 9 (2).

———. 2016b. *The Socially Inclusive Role of Curatorial Voice: A Qualitative Comparative Study of the Use of Gatekeeping Mechanisms and the Co-Creation of Identity in Museums*. Tallahassee: Florida State University.

Coleman, Laura-Edythe, and Porchia Moore. Forthcoming. "Where Is Your Office? Social Justice Advocacy and the American Grass Roots Museum Professionals' Movement." In *Museums and Activism*. Edited by Robert Janes and Richard Sandell. New York: Routledge.

Coleman, Laura-Edythe, Porchia Moore, Rose Paquet-Kinsley, and Alethia Wittman. 2016. "The Socially Inclusive Museum: Perspectives from American Museum Researchers and Professionals."

Creswell, John W. 2009. *Research Design: Qualitative, Quantitative, and Mixed Methods Approaches*, 3rd ed. Thousand Oaks, CA: Sage.

———. 2013. *Qualitative Inquiry and Research Design: Choosing among Five Approaches*. Los Angeles: Sage.

CUNY. *Citizenship Now!*

Dana, John Cotton. 1917. *The New Museum*. Woodstock, VT: Elm Tree Press.

Davies, William. 2017. "How Statistics Lost Their Power—and Why We Should Fear What Comes Next." *The Guardian*, January 19. https://www.theguardian.com/politics/2017/jan/19/crisis-of-statistics-big-data-democracy.

Denniston, Helen, Eric Langham, and Emma Martin. 2003. *Holding Up the Mirror: Addressing Cultural Diversity in London's Museum*. London: London Museums Agency.

Denver Foundation. "Inclusiveness at Work: How to Build Inclusive Nonprofit Organizations." http://www.nonprofitinclusiveness.org/inclusiveness-work-how-build-inclusive-nonprofit-organizations.

Department for Culture, Media and Sport. 2000. *Policy Guidance on Social Inclusion for DCMS Funded and Local Authority Museums, Galleries and Archives in England*.

DiMaggio, Paul, and Francie Ostrower. 1990. "Participation in the Arts by Black and White Americans." *Social Forces* 68 (3): 753–78. doi:10.1093/sf/68.3.753.

Dodd, Jocelyn, Helen O'Riain, Eilean Hooper-Greenhill, Richard San-
dell, Heritage Lottery Fund, and Great Britain. 2002. *A Catalyst for
Change: The Social Impact of the Open Museum*. Leicester, UK: Research
Centre for Museums and Galleries.

Dodd, Jocelyn, and Richard Sandell. 2001. *Including Museums: Perspectives on Museums, Galleries and Social Inclusion*. Leicester, UK: Research Centre for Museums and Galleries.

European Union. 2005. *The Role of Culture in Preventing and Reducing
Poverty and Social Exclusion*. Belgium: European Union.

Falk, John H. 2009. *Identity and the Museum Visitor Experience*. Walnut
Creek, CA: Left Coast Press.

Falk, John H., and Lynn D. Dierking. 1992. *The Museum Experience*.
Washington, DC: Whalesback Books.

———. 2000. *Learning from Museums: Visitor Experiences and the Making
of Meaning*. American Association for State and Local History Book
Series. Walnut Creek, CA: AltaMira Press.

Falk, John H., Joseph Heimlich, and Kerry Bronnenkant. 2008. "Us-
ing Identity-Related Visit Motivations as a Tool for Understanding
Adult Zoo and Aquarium Visitors' Meaning-Making." *Curator: The
Museum Journal* 51 (1): 55–79.

Falk, John H., John J. Koran, Lynn D. Dierking, and Lewis Dreblow.
2010. "Predicting Visitor Behavior." *Curator: The Museum Journal* 28
(4): 249–58.

Fletcher, Kami. 2016. *#MuseumsRespondtoFerguson: An Interview with
Aleia Brown and Adrianne Russell—AAIHS*. http://www.aaihs.org/
museumsrespondtoferguson-an-interview-with-aleia-brown-and
-adrianne-russell/.

Fortin, Jacey. 2017. "The Statue at the Center of Charlottesville's
Storm." *New York Times*, August 13. https://www.nytimes.com/
2017/08/13/us/charlottesville-rally-protest-statue.html.

Fuhrmans, Christoph, and Scott Blumenthal. 2017. "An Artistic Approach to Becoming a U.S. Citizen." *New York Times*, October
25. https://www.nytimes.com/interactive/2017/10/25/arts/ny
-historical-society-citizenship-program.html.

Griffiths, Jose-Marie, and Donald King. 2008. *InterConnections: The
IMLS National Study on the Use of Libraries, Museums, and the Internet*.

Grootaert, Christiaan, Deepa Narayam, Veronica Nyhan Jones, and
Michael Woolcock. 2004. *Measuring Social Capital: An Integrated
Questionnaire*. World Bank Working Paper. Washington, DC: World
Bank.

Group for Large Local Authority Museums. 2000. *Museums and Social Inclusion: The GLLAM Report.* Leicester, UK: Research Centre for Museums and Galleries.

Hood, Marilyn. 1983. "Staying Away: Why People Choose Not to Visit Museums." *Museum News* 61 (4): 50–57.

Incluseum. "Incluseum: About Us." Accessed June 1, 2017. https://incluseum.com/about/.

Inclusive Museum. "The Inclusive Museum." http://onmuseums.com/the-conference.

International Council of Museums. 2007. *Museum Definition.* http://icom.museum/the-vision/museum-definition/.

Jacobsen, John W. 2014. "The Community Service Museum: Owning Up to Our Multiple Missions." *Museum Management and Curatorship* 29 (1): 1–18. doi:10.1080/09647775.2013.869851.

Janes, Robert R. 2009. *Museums in a Troubled World: Renewal, Irrelevance or Collapse?* Museum Meanings. London; New York: Routledge.

Jung, Yuha. 2016. "Contemporary Understanding of 'Harlem on My Mind': What Can We Learn from an Art Museum's Early Attempt toward Culturally Inclusive Practice?" *International Journal of the Inclusive Museum* 10 (1): 41–50.

Karp, Ivan, and Steven Lavine. 1991. *Exhibiting Cultures: The Poetics and Politics of Museum Display.* Edited by Rockefeller Foundation. Washington, DC: Smithsonian Institution Press.

Kelly, Lynda. 2005. "Evaluation, Research and Communities of Practice: Program Evaluation in Museums." *Archival Science* 4 (1–2): 45–69.

———. 2006. "Measuring the Impact of Museums on Their Communities—Australian Museum." International Council on Museums, November 2, 2006.

Levy, Nicole. "Museum to Prep Would-Be U.S. Citizens with Scavenger Hunt, Exhibitions." Accessed October 28, 2017. https://www.dnainfo.com/new-york/20170420/upper-west-side/new-york-historical-society-cuny-citizenship-project-green-card-naturalization.

Lincoln, Abraham. 1863. *Gettysburg Address.*

McCarthy, Catherine, and Brad Herring. 2015. "Museums & Community Partnerships: Collaboration Guide for Museums Working with Community Youth-Serving Organizations." http://www.nisenet.org/sites/default/files/NISE%20Network%20Collaboration%20Guide%2011-20-2015%20FINAL.pdf.

Middleton, Margaret. 2014. "Including the 21st Century Family." Incluseum, July 7. Accessed July 7, 2017. https://incluseum.com/2014/07/07/including-the-21st-century-family/.

———. 2017. "Barbie Gets with the Program, 2017." Accessed November 4, 2017. https://www.behance.net/gallery/51088635/Barbie-Gets-With-the-Program-2017.

Miller, William, and Benjamin Crabtree. 2004. "Depth Interviewing." In *Approaches to Qualitative Research: A Reader on Theory and Practice.* Edited by Sharlene Nagy Hesse-Biber and Patricia Leavy. New York: Oxford University Press.

Montgomery, Monica. "Museum of Impact." Accessed August 11, 2017. https://www.museumofimpact.org.

Moore, Porchia. 2014. *The Danger of the "D" Word: Museums and Diversity.* Incluseum, January 20. https://incluseum.com/2014/01/20/the-danger-of-the-d-word-museums-and-diversity/.

Moore, Porchia, and nikhil trivedi. "Visitors of Color." Accessed November 4, 2017. http://visitorsofcolor.tumblr.com/?og=1.

Murawski, Mike. 2017a. *Changing the Things We Cannot Accept — Museum Edition.* Art Museum Teaching. https://artmuseumteaching.com/tag/inclusion/.

———. 2017b. *Inclusion.* Art Museum Teaching. https://artmuseumteaching.com/tag/inclusion/.

———. 2017c. *Museums Are Not Neutral.* Art Museum Teaching. https://artmuseumteaching.com/2017/08/31/museums-are-not-neutral/.

Museum as Site for Social Action. 2017. Directed by Elisabeth Callihan. https://vimeo.com/237568276.

Museums Workers Speak. 2015. "How Do We Turn the Social Justice Lens Inward? A Conversation about Internal Museum Labor Practices." Incluseum, April 28.

National Center for Civil and Human Rights. 2014. *Way Finding Guide: Center for Civil and Human Rights.*

———. 2015. *Across Generations: Intergenerational Conversation Starters.*

New-York Historical Society. "New-York Historical Society: About." http://www.nyhistory.org/about.

———. "New-York Historical Society: The Citizenship Project." http://www.nyhistory.org/education/citizenship-project.

Oakley, K., and R. Naylor. 2005. *New Directions in Social Policy: Developing the Evidence Base for Museums, Libraries and Archives in England.* London: Museums and Libraries Archive.

Obama, Michelle. 2015. *Remarks by the First Lady at the Opening of the Whitney Museum.* New York.

Orloff, Chet. 2017. "Should Museums Change Our Mission and Become Agencies of Social Justice?" *Curator: The Museum Journal* 60 (1): 33–36.

Paquet Kinsley, Rose, and Aletheia Wittman. 2016. "Bringing Self-Examination to the Center of Social Justice Work in Museums." http://www.aam-us.org/docs/default-source/resource-library/bringing-self-examination-to-the-center-of-social-justice-work-in-museums.pdf?sfvrsn=0.

Paquet Kinsley, Rose, Aletheia Wittman, and Porchia Moore. 2014. "Joint Statement from Museum Bloggers and Colleagues on Ferguson and Related Events." Incluseum, December 22. Accessed October 10, 2015. https://incluseum.com/2014/12/22/joint-statement-from-museum-bloggers-colleagues-on-ferguson-related-events/.

Phillip, Abby. 2015. "Why Bree Newsome Took Down the Confederate Flag in S.C.: 'I Refuse to Be Ruled by Fear.'" *Washington Post*, June 29. https://www.washingtonpost.com/news/post-nation/wp/2015/06/29/why-bree-newsome-took-down-the-confederate-flag-in-s-c-i-refuse-to-be-ruled-by-fear/.

Portland Art Museum. "Mission." Accessed October 26, 2017. https://portlandartmuseum.org/about/mission/.

Rampell, Catherine. 2017. "Opinion | Huge Distrust in Government Statistics, Especially among Republicans." *Washington Post*, March 24. Accessed October 9, 2017. https://www.washingtonpost.com/news/rampage/wp/2017/03/24/huge-distrust-in-government-statistics-especially-among-republicans/.

Rawal, Nabin. 2008. "Social Inclusion and Exclusion: A Review." *Dhaulagiri Journal of Sociology and Anthropology* 2: 161–78.

Sandell, R. 1998. "Museums as Agents of Social Inclusion." *Museum Management and Curatorship* 17 (4): 401–18.

———. 2003. "Social Inclusion, the Museum and the Dynamics of Sectoral Change." *Museum and Society* 1 (1): 45–62.

Sandell, Richard, and Eithne Nightingale. 2012. *Museums, Equality, and Social Justice*. Museum Meanings. New York: Routledge.

Schonfeld, Roger, Mariet Westermann, and Liam Sweeney. 2015. *The Andrew W. Mellon Foundation Art Museum Staff Demographic Survey*. New York: Andrew W. Mellon Foundation.

Scott, Carol. 2013. *Museums and Public Value: Creating Sustainable Futures*. Edited by Carol Scott. Farnham, Surrey, UK: Ashgate.

Seidman, Irving. 1998. *Interviewing as Qualitative Research: A Guide for Researchers in Education and the Social Sciences*, 2nd ed. New York: Teachers College Press.

Serrell, Beverly. 1996. *Exhibit Labels: An Interpretive Approach*. Walnut Creek, CA: AltaMira Press.

Silver, Hilary. 1994. "Social Exclusion and Social Solidarity: Three Paradigms." *International Labour Review* 133 (5–6): 531–78.

Silverman, Lois. 2010. *The Social Work of Museums*. London: Routledge.

Simon, Nina. 2010. *The Participatory Museum*. Santa Cruz, CA: Museum 2.0.

———. 2015. *Fighting for Inclusion*. Museum 2.0. http://museumtwo.blogspot.com/2015/09/fighting-for-inclusion.html.

Spoehr, John. 2007. *Measuring Social Inclusion and Exclusion in Northern Adelaide: A Report for the Department of Health*. Adelaide: SA Dept of Health.

Sutton, Brett. 1993. "The Rationale for Qualitative Research: A Review of Principles and Theoretical Foundations." *Library Quarterly* 63 (4): 411–30.

Taylor, Chris. 2015. *Announcing the Department of Inclusion and Community Engagement at the Minnesota Historical Society: Part I*. The Incluseum. https://incluseum.com/2015/04/21/announcing-the-department-of-inclusion-and-community-engagement-at-the-minnesota-historical-society-part-i/.

Tlili, A. 2008. "Behind the Policy Mantra of the Inclusive Museum: Receptions of Social Exclusion and Inclusion in Museums and Science Centres." *Cultural Sociology* 2 (1): 123–47.

trivedi, nikhil. 2015. *Text from My Ignite Talk at MCN 2015*. http://nikhiltrivedi.com/2015/11/05/text-from-my-ignite-talk-at-mcn-2015.html.

UK Museums Association. 2014. *Valuing Diversity: The Case for Inclusive Museums*.

United Way. "Diversity and Inclusion | United Way Worldwide." Accessed September 25, 2017. https://www.unitedway.org/about/diversity-and-inclusion.

University of Leicester. "Socially Engaged Practice in Museums and Galleries." Accessed July 20, 2017. https://le.ac.uk/courses/socially-engaged-practice-in-museums-and-galleries-ma-msc-dl.

US Census Bureau. "New Census Data Show Differences between Urban and Rural Populations." Accessed October 24, 2017. https://www.census.gov/newsroom/press-releases/2016/cb16-210.html.

US Government. 2015. "U.S. Commission on Civil Rights Celebrates the 25th Anniversary of the Americans with Disabilities Act of 1990." *Politics & Government Business* 55.

Voon, Claire. "New York-Historical Society Offers Workshops for US Residents Seeking Citizenship." Accessed October 28, 2017. https://hyperallergic.com/373036/new-york-historical-society-offers-workshops-for-us-residents-seeking-citizenship/.

Wecker, Menachem. 2015. "At Some Museums, Blind Visitors Can Touch the Art." *Washington Post*, July 9. Accessed October 24, 2017. https://www.washingtonpost.com/entertainment/museums/at-some -museums-blind-visitors-can-touch-the-art/2015/07/09/df4a5bba -fd6d-11e4-833c-a2de05b6b2a4_story.html.

Weil, Stephen. 1999. "Transformed from a Cemetery of Bric-a-Brac." *Perspectives on Outcome Based Evaluation for Libraries and Museums.*

———. 2002. *Making Museums Matter.* Washington, DC: Smithsonian Institution Press.

West, Celine, and Charlotte H. F. Smith. 2005. "'We Are Not a Government Poodle': Museums and Social Inclusion under New Labour." *International Journal of Government Policy* 11 (3): 275–88.

Wilson, Lou. 2006. "Developing a Model for the Measurement of Social Inclusion and Social Capital in Regional Australia." *Social Indicators Research* 75 (3): 335–60.

Index

About the Author

Laura-Edythe Coleman, PhD, is a museum informaticist specializing in social inclusion theory and practice. Her focus is on the point of convergence for museums, information, people, and technology. Knowing that societies need museums for creating and sustaining cultural memory, she strives to help communities co-create collections with museums. She is currently a lecturer for the Johns Hopkins University museum studies program, in which she teaches two core courses: "Museums in a Global Perspective" and "The History and Philosophy of Museums."

She holds a PhD in information science, a master's of library and information science, and a bachelor's of fine arts. She brings an extensive background in cultural heritage informatics, LIS education, and information technology to focus on cultural institutions that are embedded in communities reconciling civil conflict. Her motto is "save the world: one object, one exhibit, one museum, one community, one nation at a time." She can be reached via Twitter (@lauraedythe), website (www.lauraedythe.com), or email (lauraedythecoleman@gmail.com).